FOR ORGANS, PIANOS & ELECTRONIC KEYBOARDS

**E-Z PLAY TODAY**

**200**

# THE BEST SONGS EVER

ISBN 0-7935-0547-X

## HAL•LEONARD® CORPORATION

7777 W. BLUEMOUND RD. P.O. BOX 13819 MILWAUKEE, WI 53213

E-Z Play® Today Music Notation © 1975 by HAL LEONARD CORPORATION

E-Z PLAY and EASY ELECTRONIC KEYBOARD MUSIC are registered trademarks of HAL LEONARD CORPORATION.

Visit Hal Leonard Online at
**www.halleonard.com**

FOR ORGANS, PIANOS & ELECTRONIC KEYBOARDS

E-Z PLAY TODAY

200

# THE BEST SONGS EVER

# All I Ask of You
## from THE PHANTOM OF THE OPERA

Registration 8
Rhythm: 8 Beat or Rock

Music by Andrew Lloyd Webber
Lyrics by Charles Hart
Additional Lyrics by Richard Stilgoe

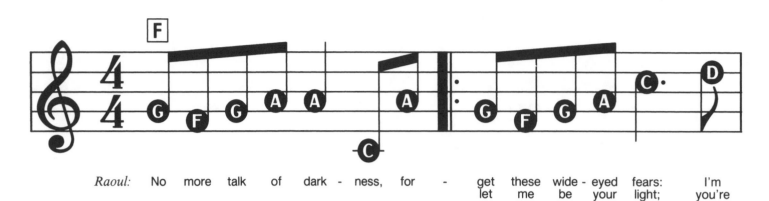

*Raoul:* No more talk of dark - ness, for - get these wide - eyed fears: I'm
let me be your light; you're

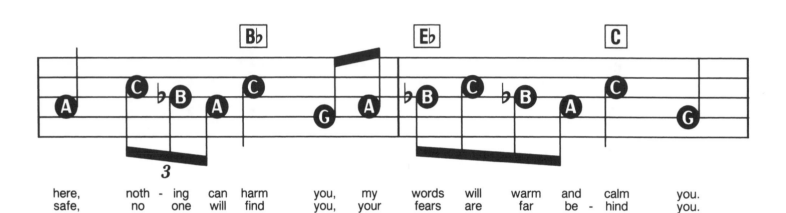

here, noth - ing can harm you, my words will warm and calm you.
safe, no one will find you, your fears are far be - hind you.

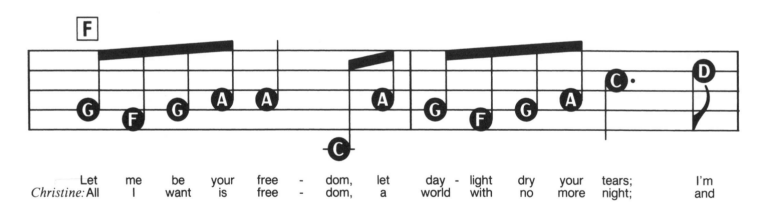

Let me be your free - dom, let day - light dry your tears; I'm
*Christine:* All I want is free - dom, a world with no more night; and

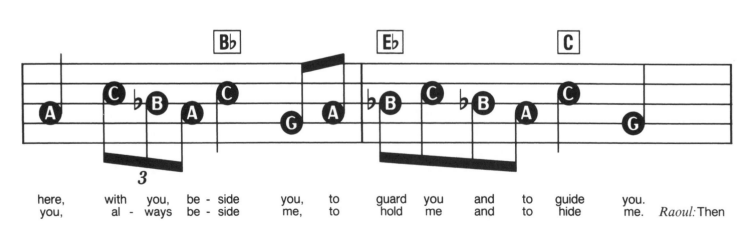

here, with you, be - side you, to guard you and to guide you.
you, al - ways be - side me, to hold me and to hide me. *Raoul:* Then

5

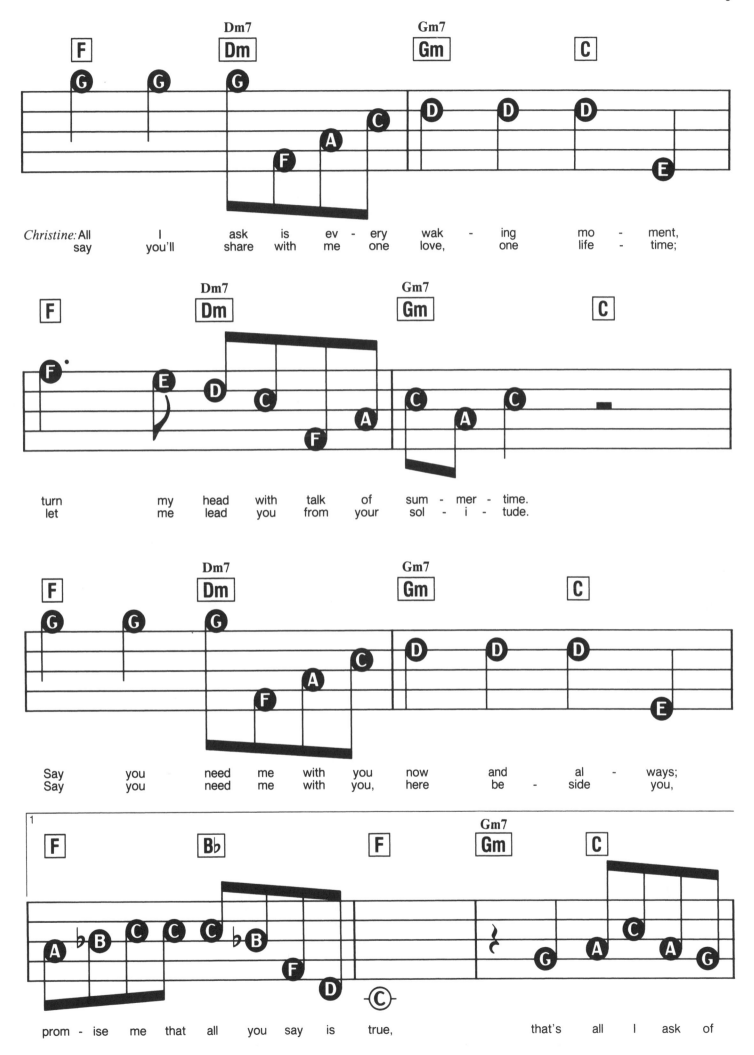

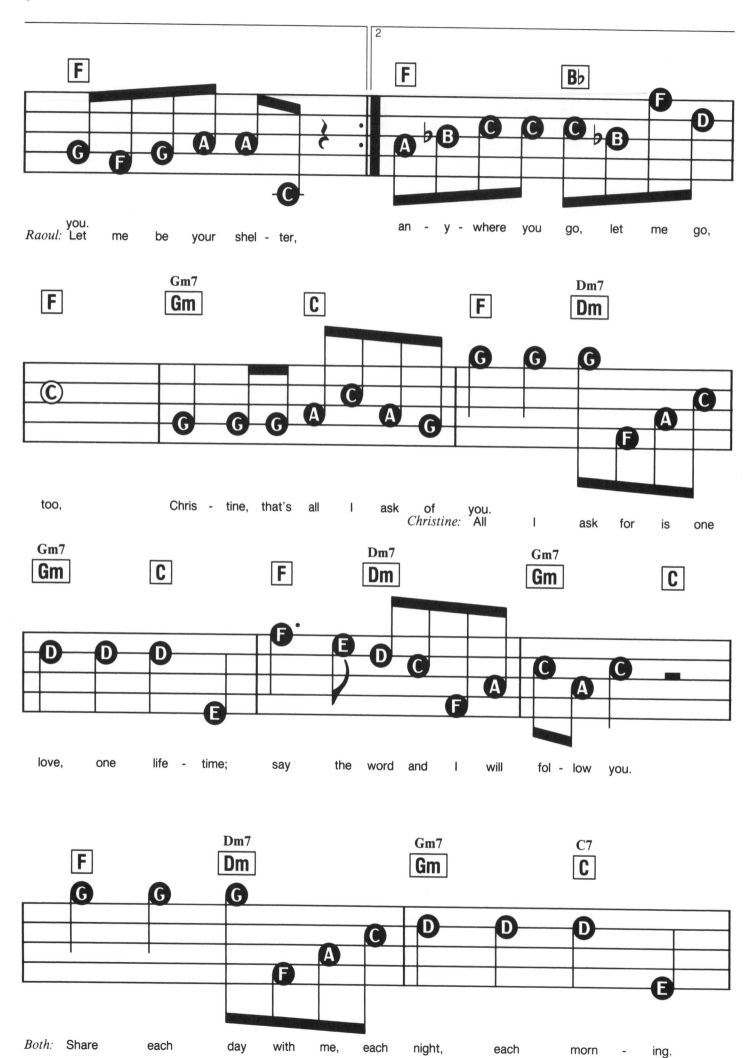

# All the Things You Are

## from VERY WARM FOR MAY

Registration 2
Rhythm: Ballad or Swing

Lyrics by Oscar Hammerstein II
Music by Jerome Kern

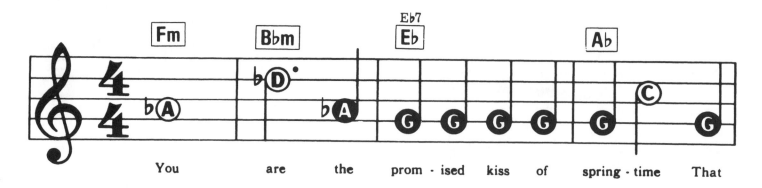

You are the prom - ised kiss of spring - time That

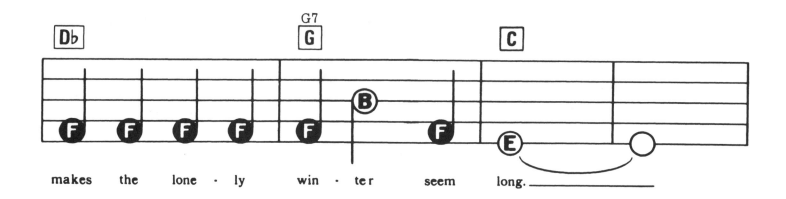

makes the lone - ly win - te r seem long._____

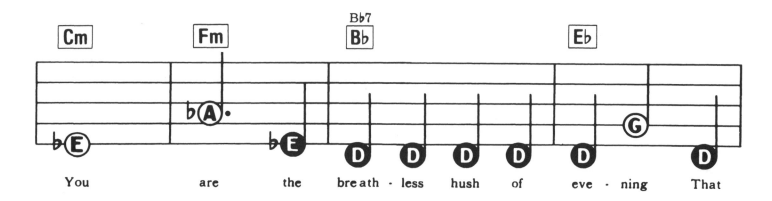

You are the breath - less hush of eve - ning That

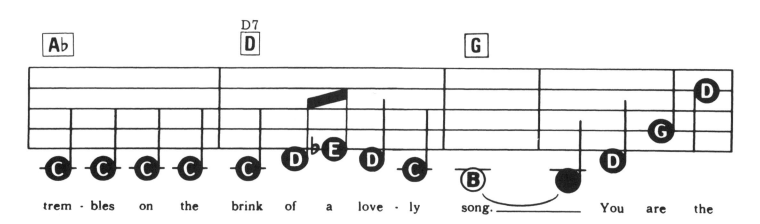

trem - bles on the brink of a love - ly song._____ You are the

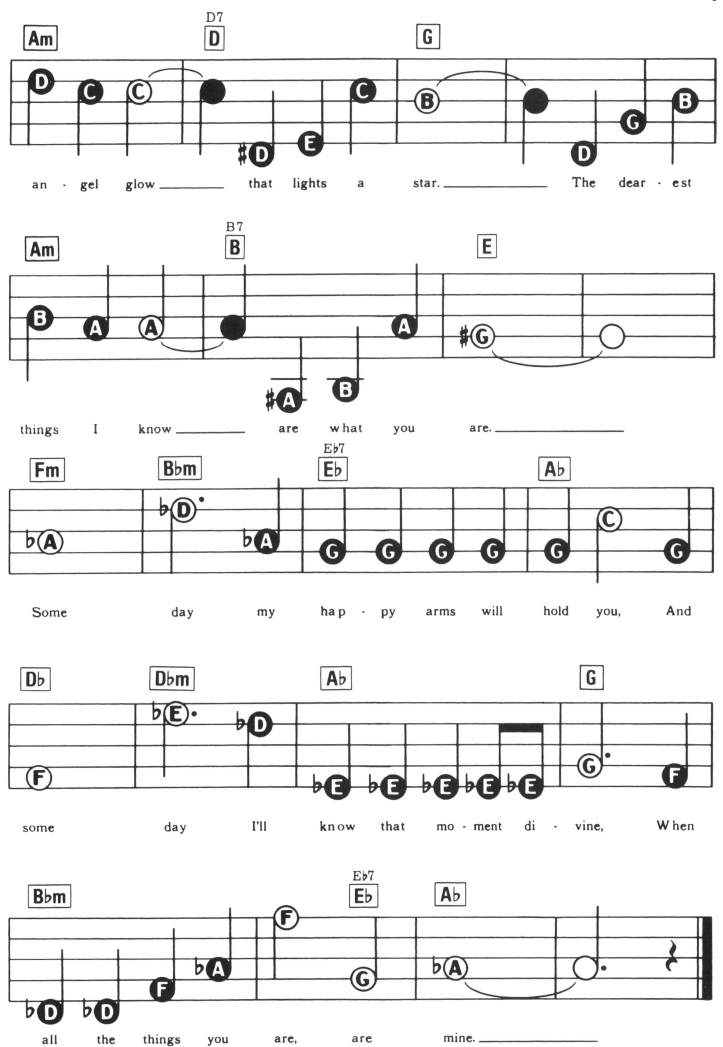

# Always

Registration 2
Rhythm: Waltz

Words and Music by
Irving Berlin

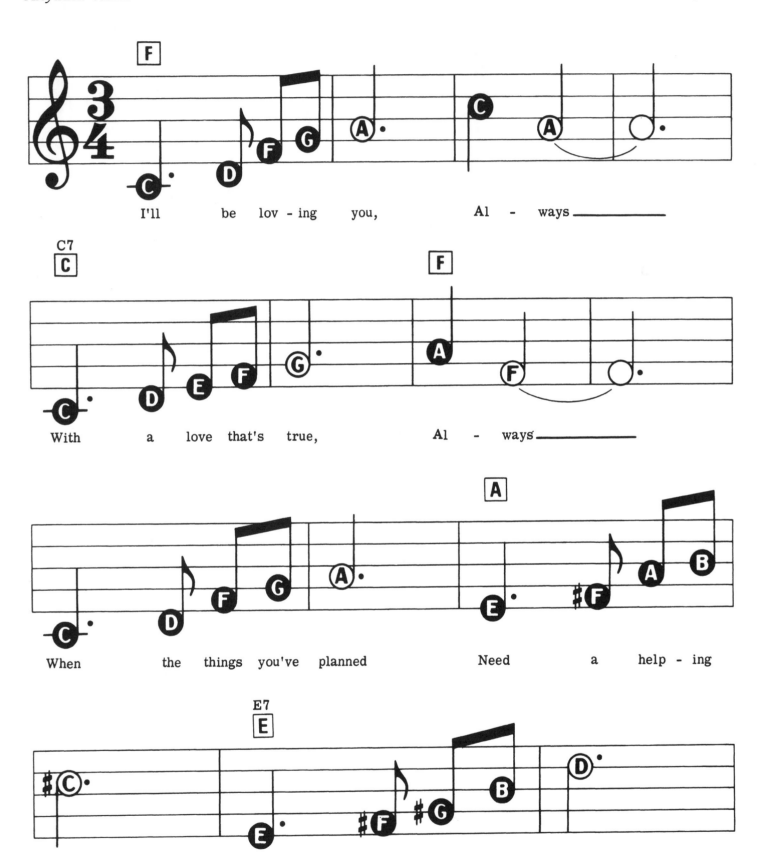

I'll    be  lov - ing  you,       Al - ways _____

With    a  love  that's  true,       Al - ways _____

When    the things you've planned    Need    a  help - ing

hand,        I   will  un - der - stand,

11

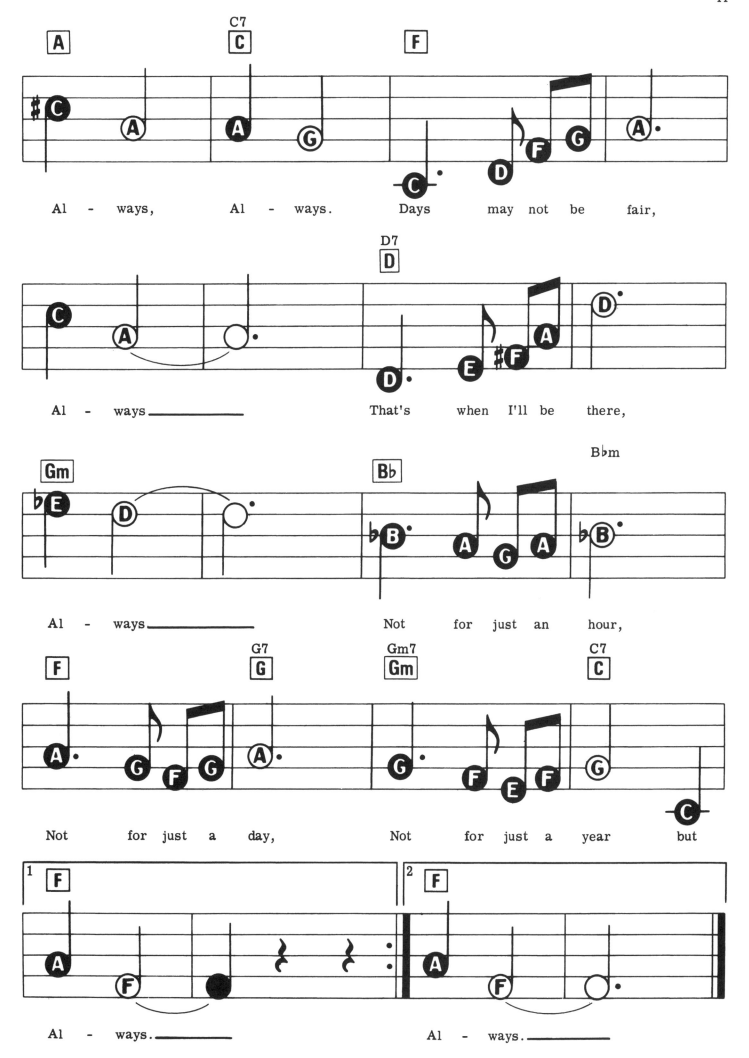

# Bewitched
## from PAL JOEY

Registration 10
Rhythm: Ballad or Fox Trot

Words by Lorenz Hart
Music by Richard Rodgers

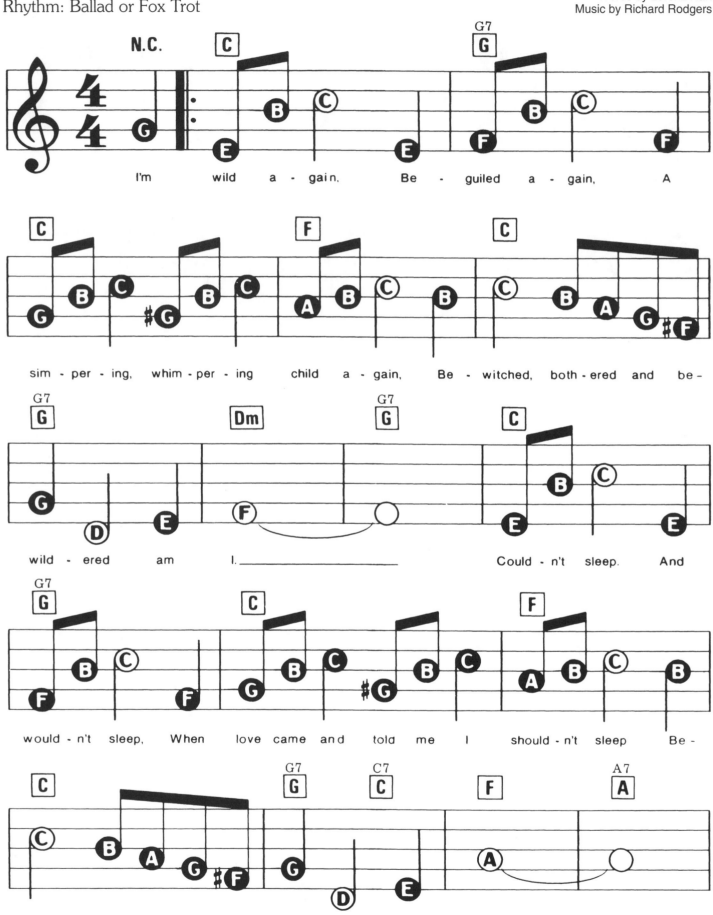

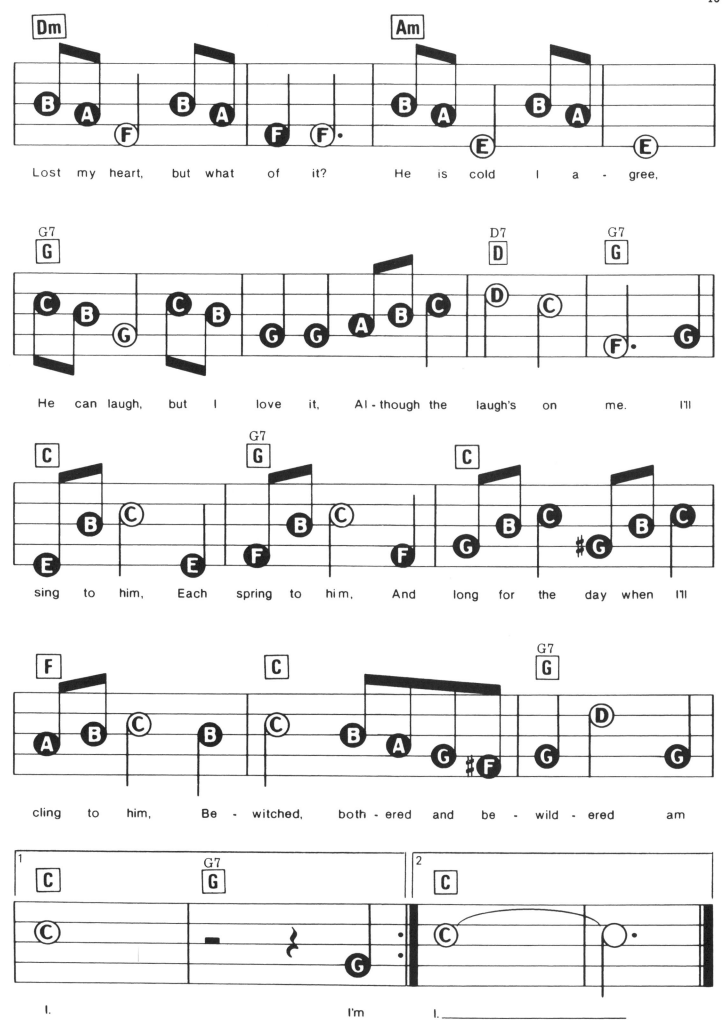

# Blue Skies
## from BETSY
## featured in BLUE SKIES

Registration 8
Rhythm: Fox Trot or Swing

Words and Music by
Irving Berlin

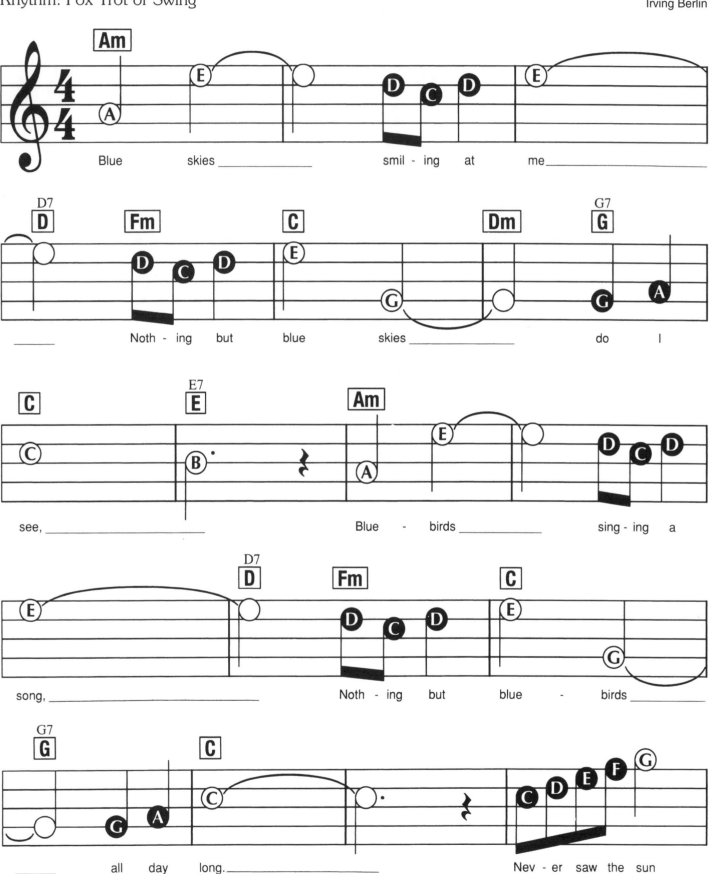

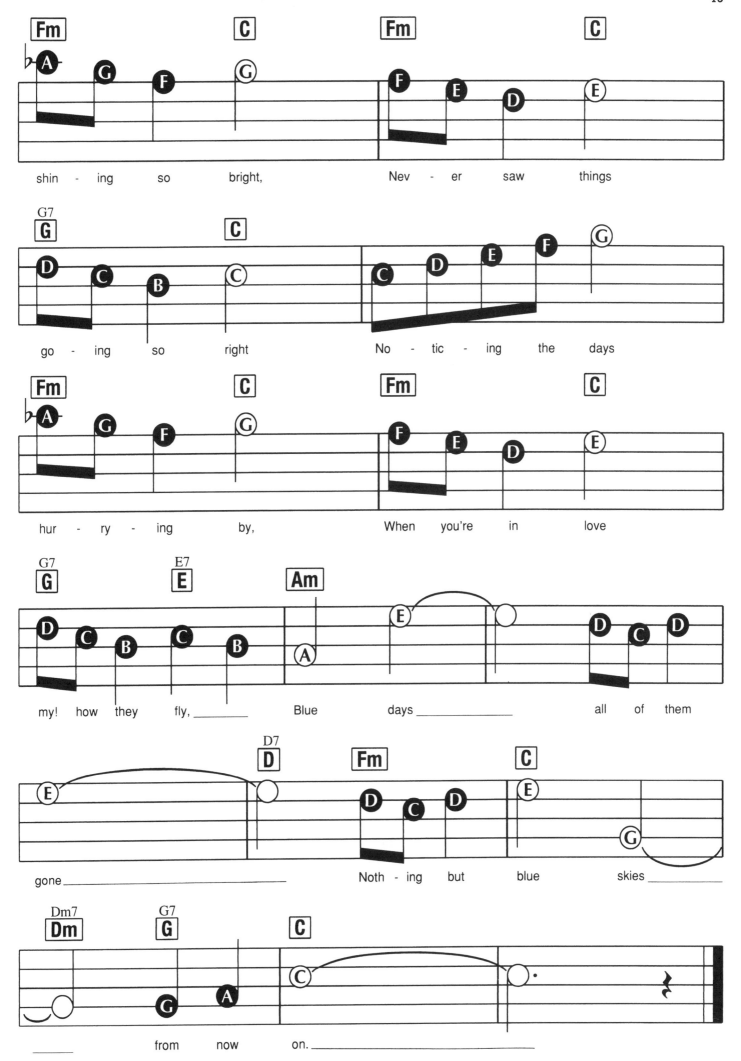

# Body and Soul

Registration 1
Rhythm: Fox Trot or Swing

Words by Edward Heyman,
Robert Sour and Frank Eyton
Music by John Green

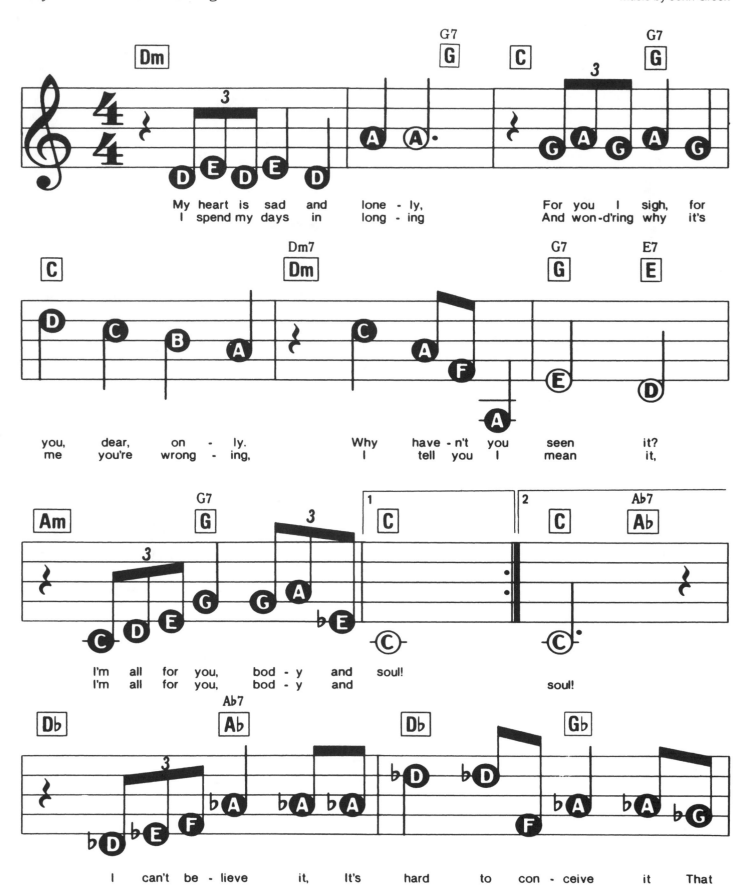

# Call Me Irresponsible

**from the Paramount Picture PAPA'S DELICATE CONDITION**

Registration 8
Rhythm: Swing

Words by Sammy Cahn
Music by James Van Heusen

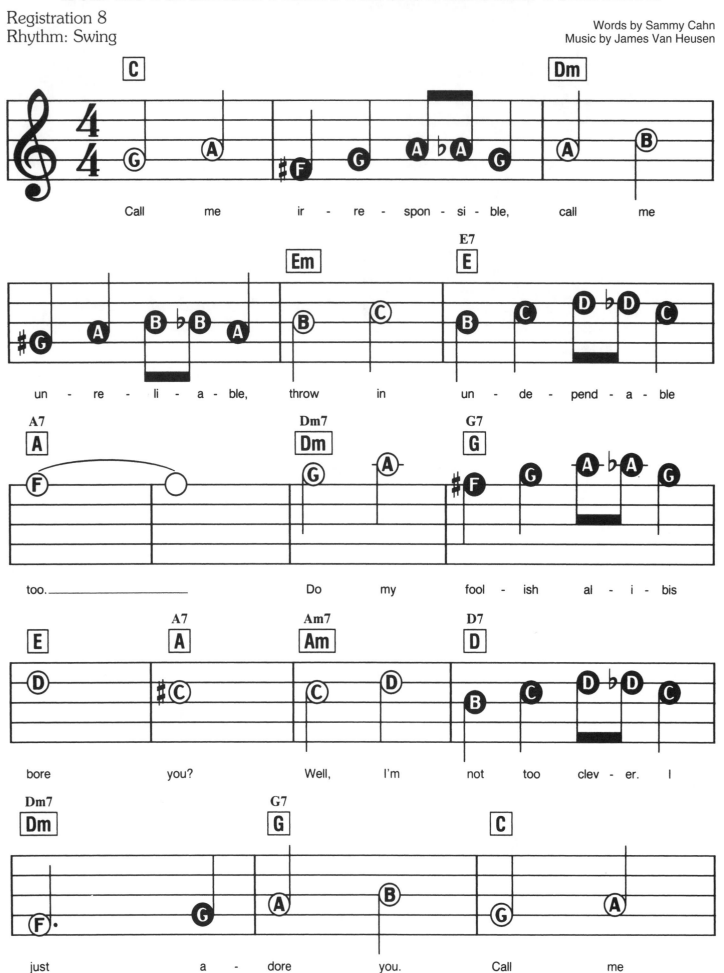

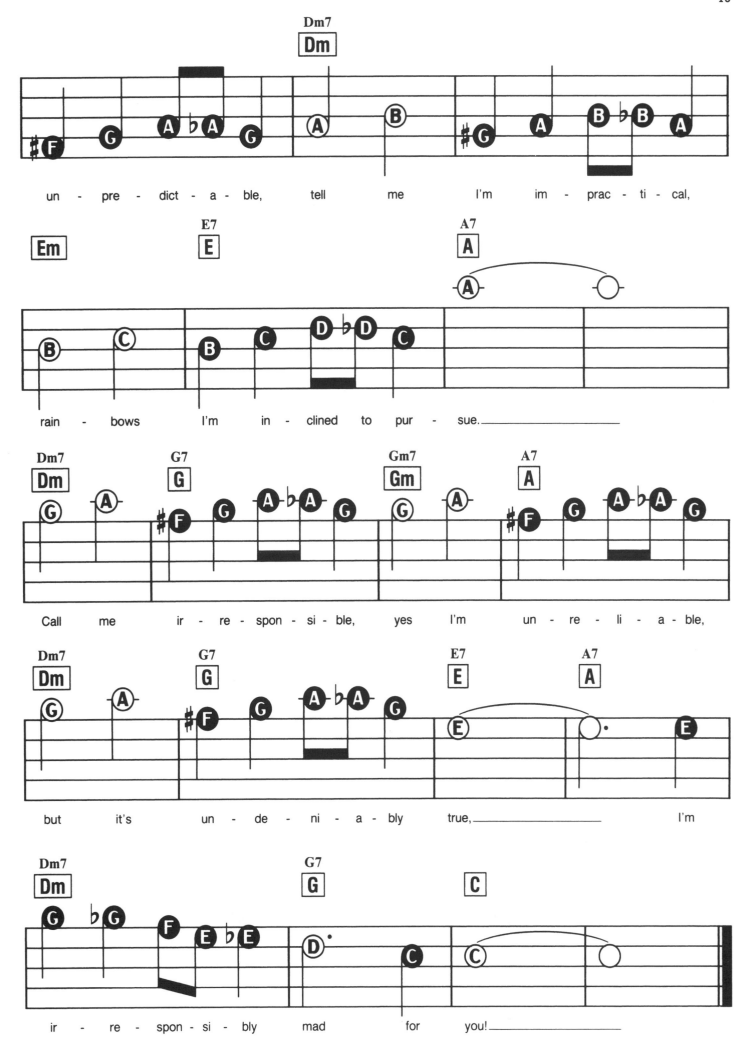

# Can't Help Falling in Love

## from the Paramount Picture BLUE HAWAII

Registration 3
Rhythm: Ballad or Swing

Words and Music by George David Weiss,
Hugo Peretti and Luigi Creatore

Wise    men    say    on - ly
Shall    I    stay?    Would    it

fools    rush    in,    but    I    can't
be    a    sin    if    I    can't

help    fall - ing    in    love    with    you.
help    fall - ing    in    love    with    you?

Like    a    riv - er    flows    sure - ly    to    the    sea,

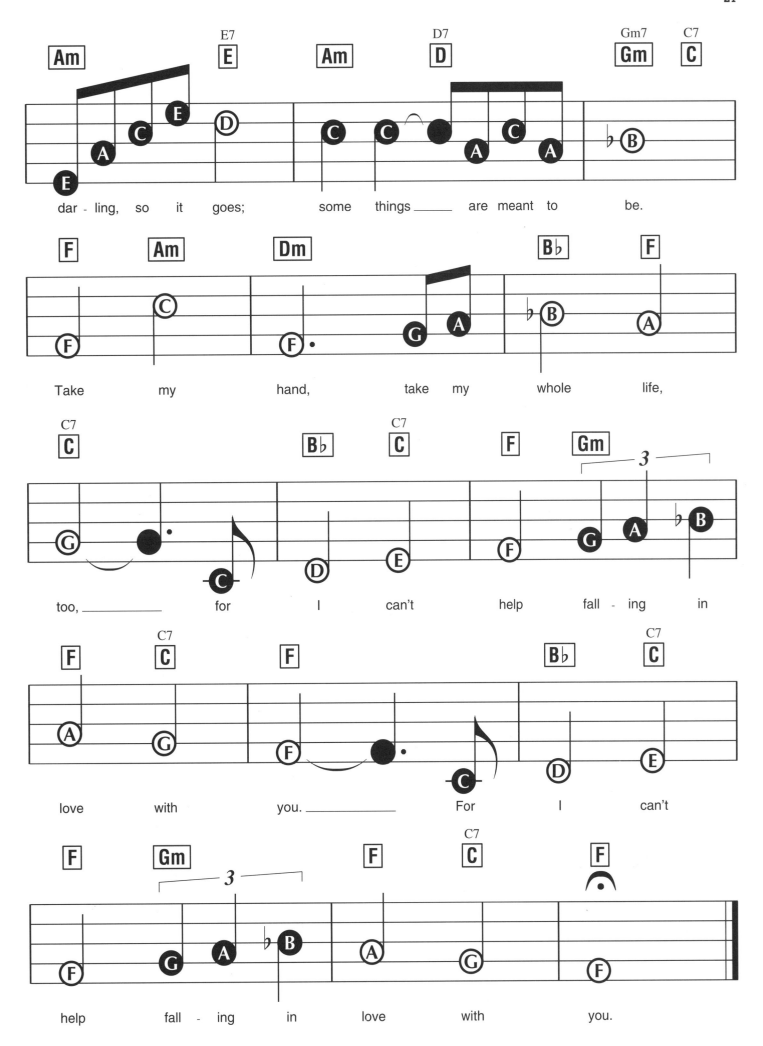

# Can You Feel the Love Tonight
## from Walt Disney Pictures' THE LION KING

Registration 2
Rhythm: Rock or 8 Beat

Music by Elton John
Lyrics by Tim Rice

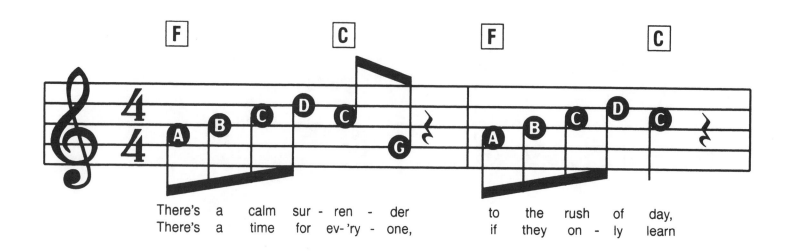

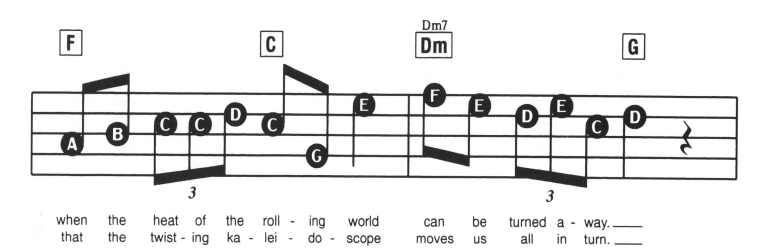

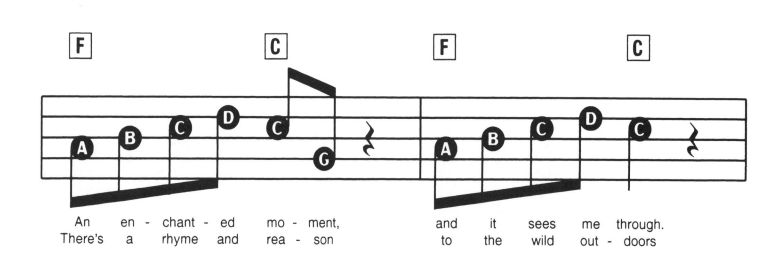

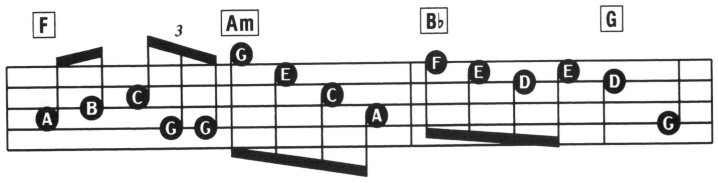

It's e - nough for this rest - less war - rior just to be with you.
when the heart of this star - crossed voy - ag - er beats in time with yours. } And

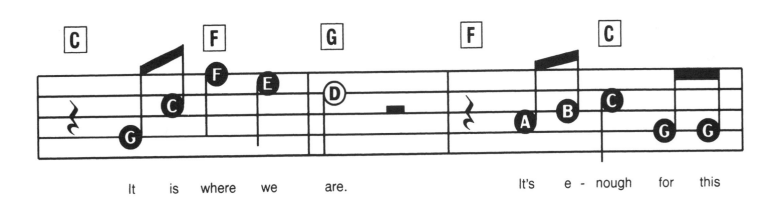

can you feel the love to - night?

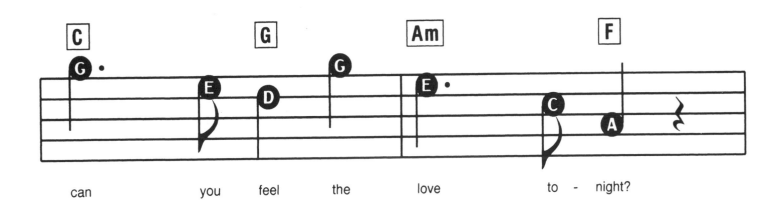

It is where we are. It's e - nough for this

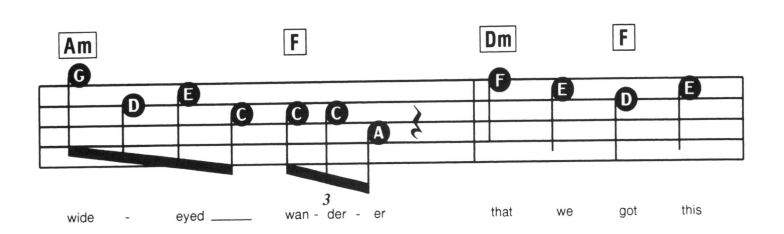

wide - eyed _____ wan - der - er that we got this

# Candle in the Wind

Registration 8
Rhythm: Rock or 8 Beat

Music by Elton John
Words by Bernie Taupin

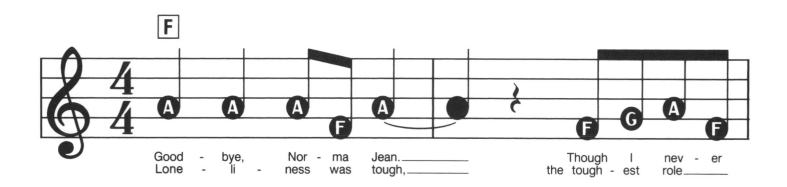

Good - bye, Nor - ma Jean._____ Though I nev - er
Lone - li - ness was tough,_____ the tough - est role

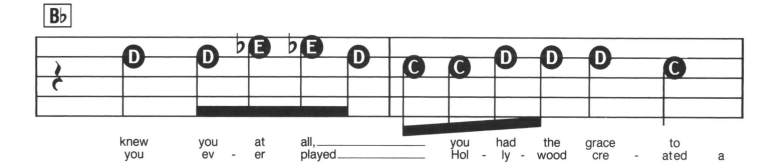

knew you at all,_____ you had the grace to
you ev - er played_____ Hol - ly - wood cre - at - ed a

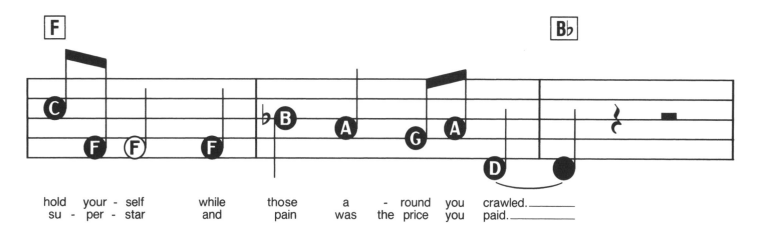

hold your - self while those a - round you crawled._____
su - per - star and pain was the price you paid._____

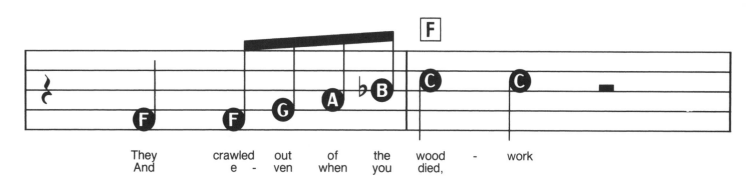

They crawled out of the wood - work
And e - ven when you died,

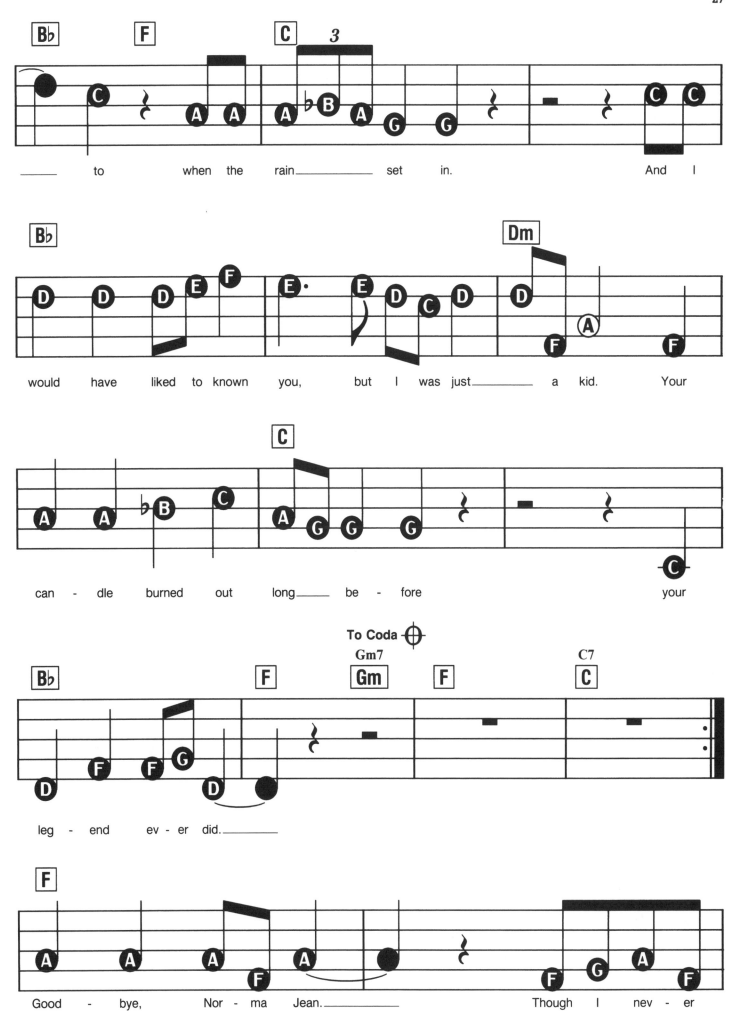

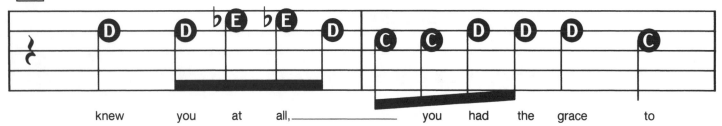

knew you at all,_____ you had the grace to

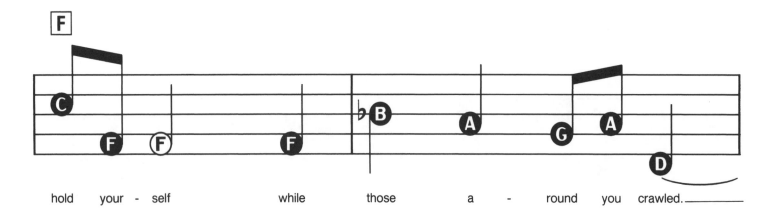

hold your - self while those a - round you crawled._____

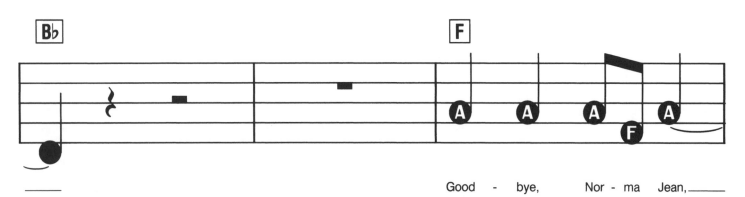

_____ Good - bye, Nor - ma Jean,_____

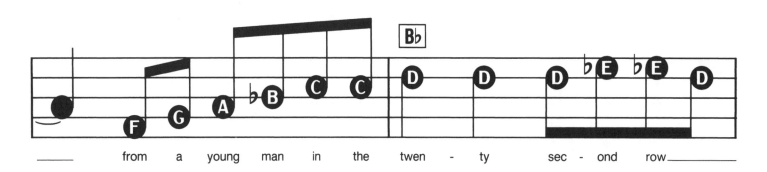

_____ from a young man in the twen - ty sec - ond row_____

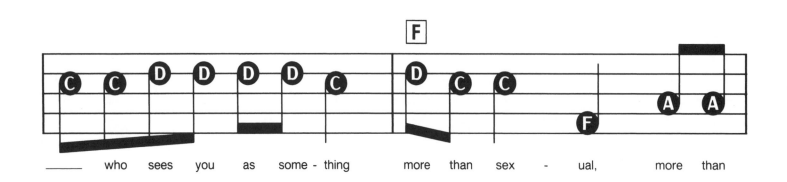

_____ who sees you as some - thing more than sex - ual, more than

**D.S. al Coda**
(Return to %
Play to ⊕ and
skip to Coda)

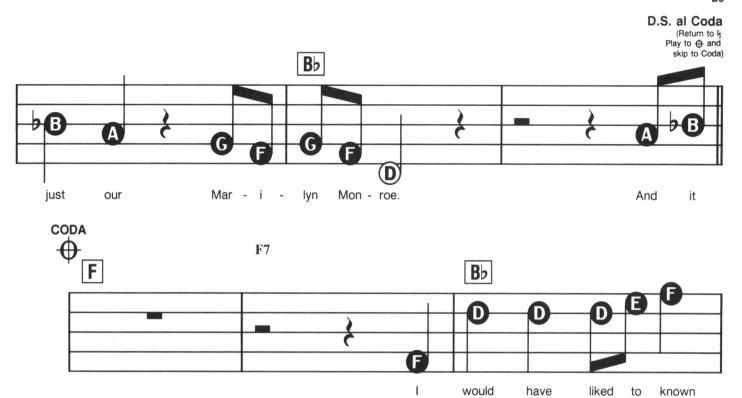

just our Mar - i - lyn Mon - roe. And it

**CODA**

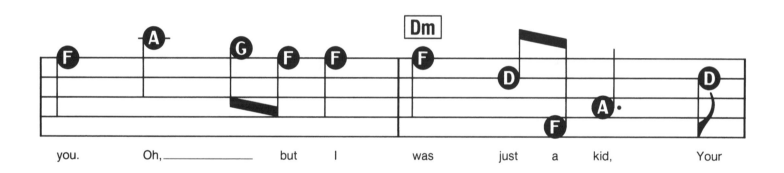

I would have liked to known

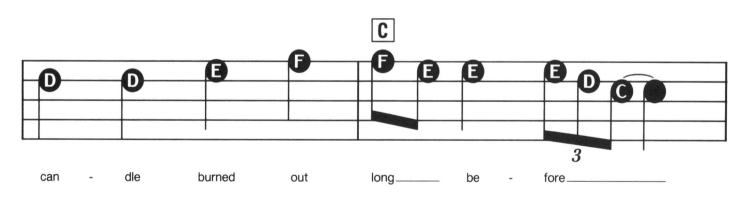

you. Oh,_____ but I was just a kid, Your

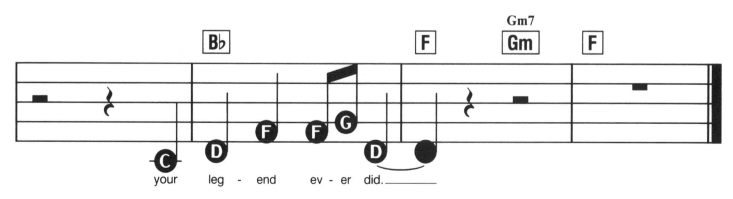

can - dle burned out long_____ be - fore_____

your leg - end ev - er did._____

# Climb Ev'ry Mountain
## from THE SOUND OF MUSIC

Registration 5
Rhythm: Swing or Fox Trot

Lyrics by Oscar Hammerstein II
Music by Richard Rodgers

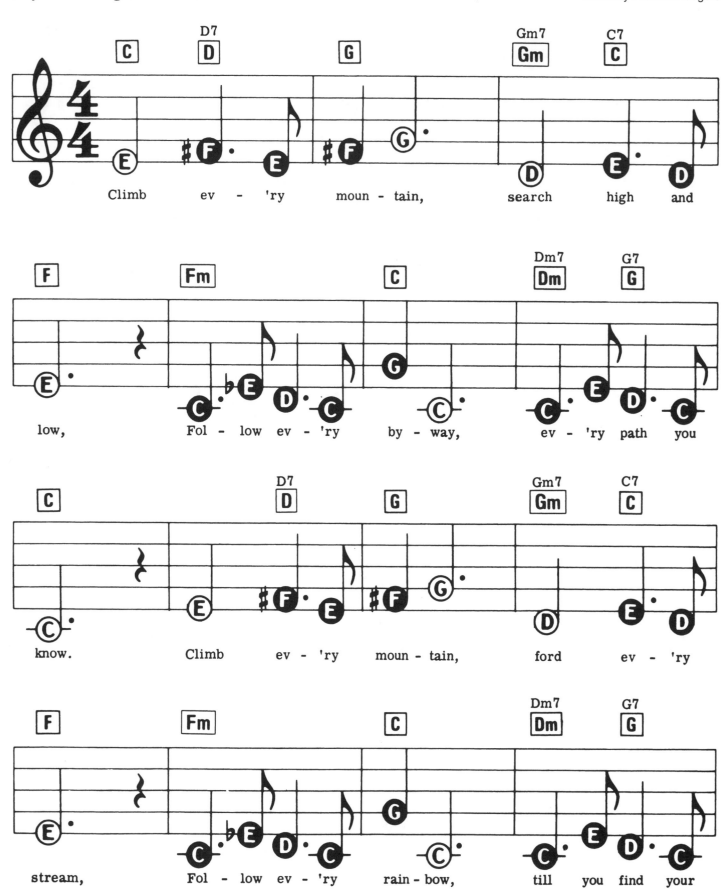

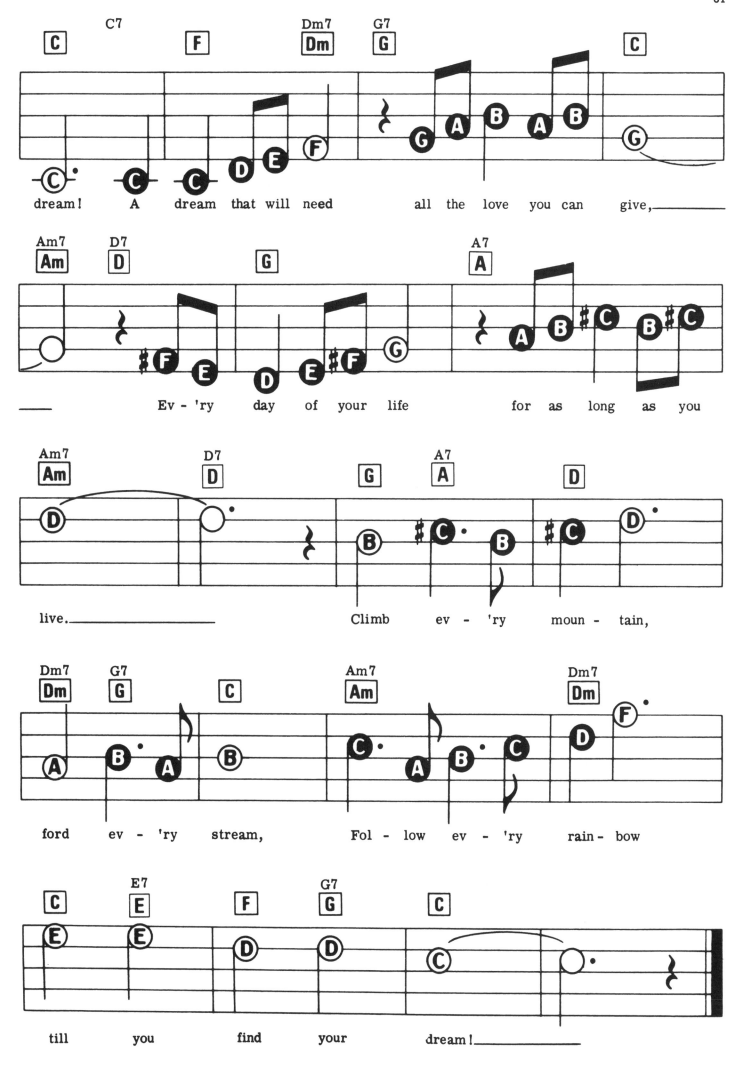

# Crazy

Registration 2
Rhythm: Fox Trot or Swing

Words and Music by
Willie Nelson

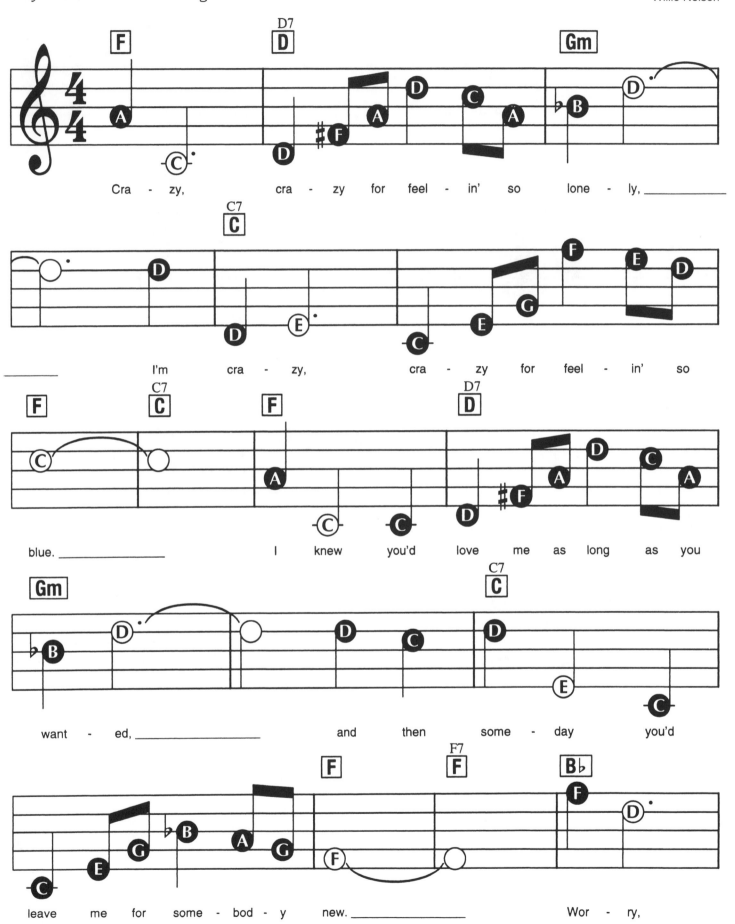

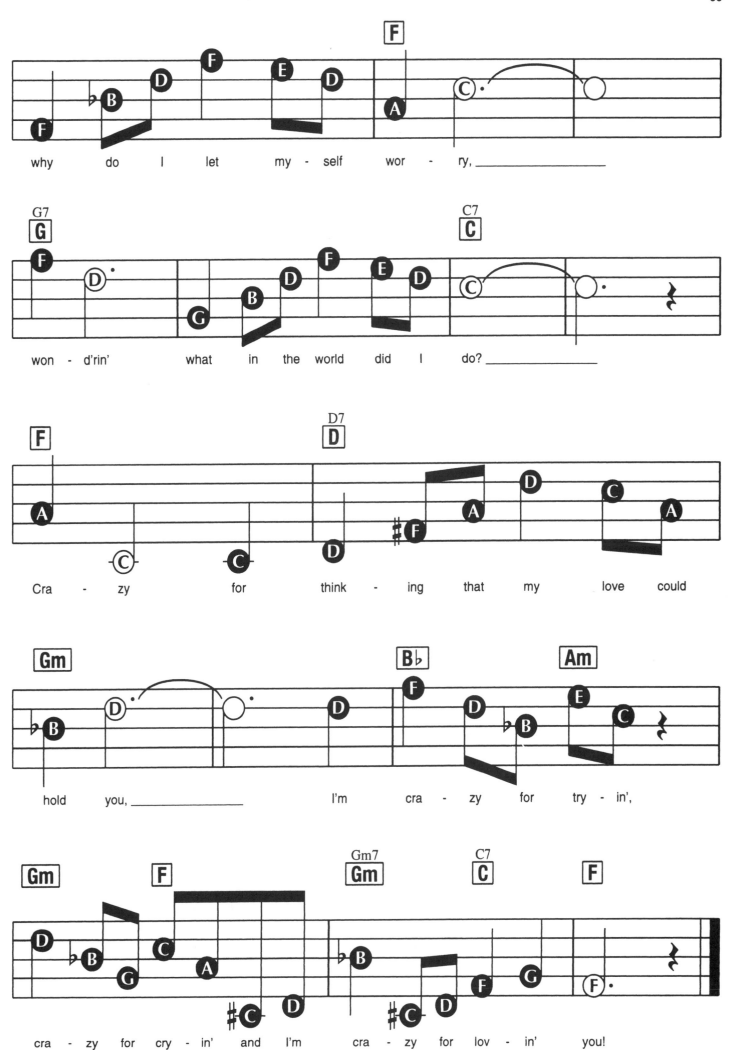

# Edelweiss
## from THE SOUND OF MUSIC

Registration 1
Rhythm: Waltz

Lyrics by Oscar Hammerstein II
Music by Richard Rodgers

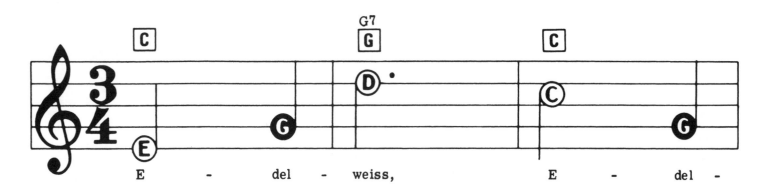

E  -  del  -  weiss,       E  -  del  -

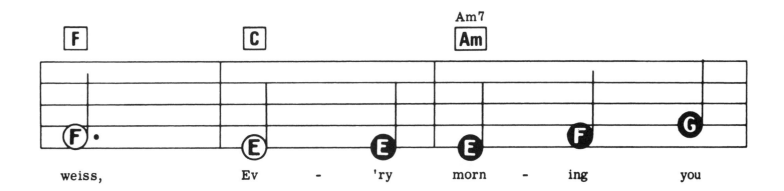

weiss,       Ev  -  'ry  morn  -  ing  you

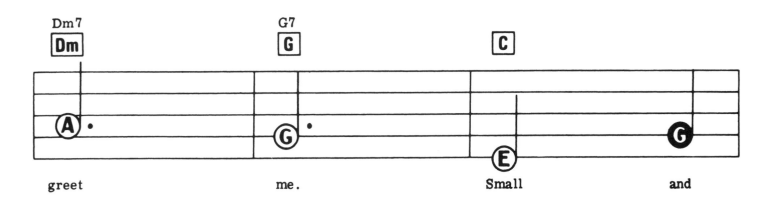

greet       me.       Small       and

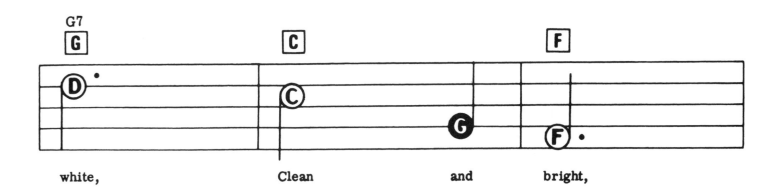

white,       Clean       and       bright,

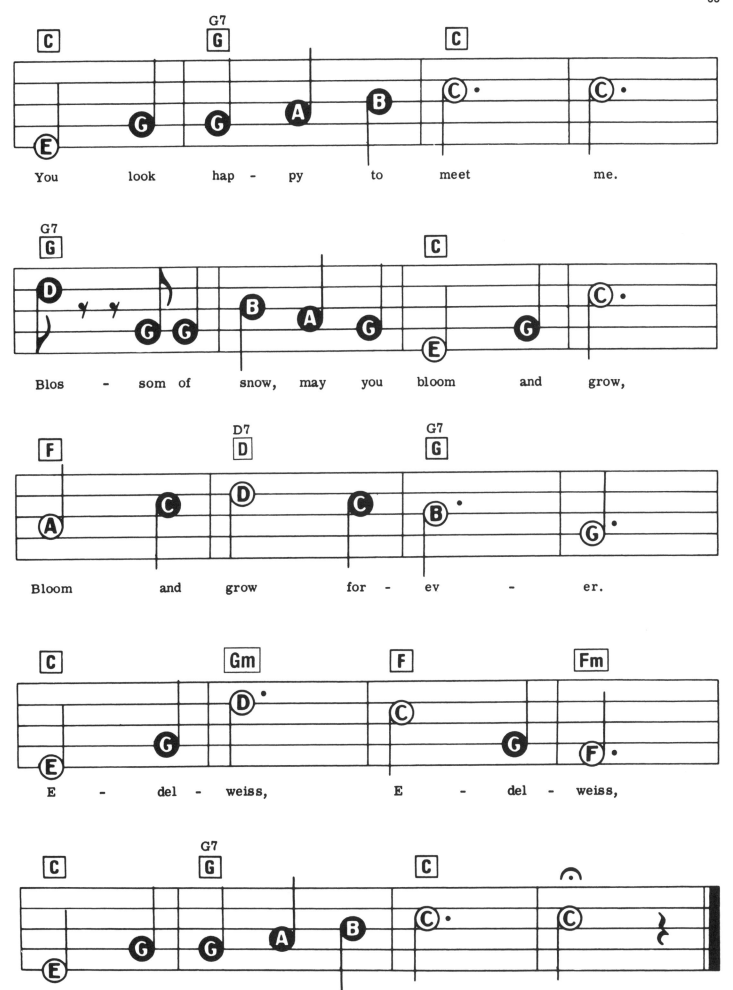

# Fly Me to the Moon
## (In Other Words)

Registration 2
Rhythm: Waltz or Jazz Waltz

Words and Music by
Bart Howard

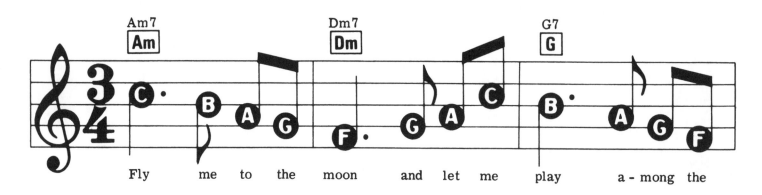

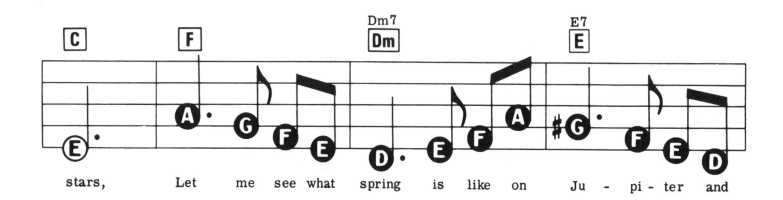

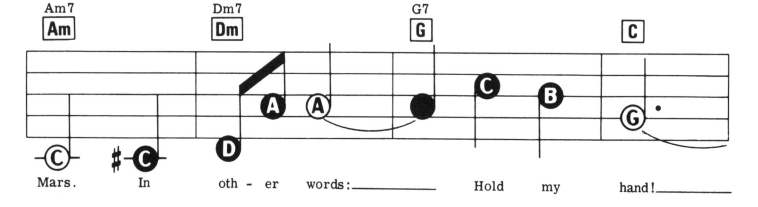

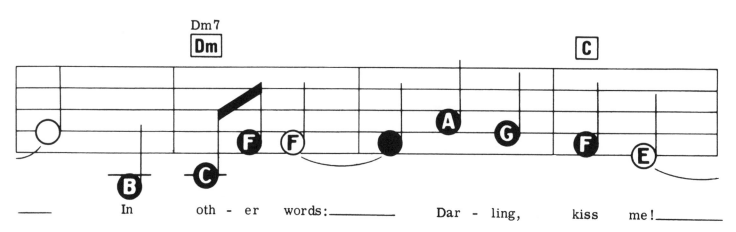

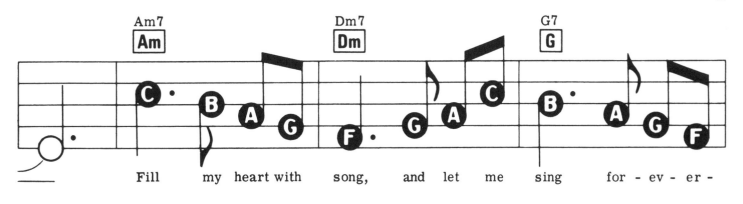

Fill my heart with song, and let me sing for - ev - er -

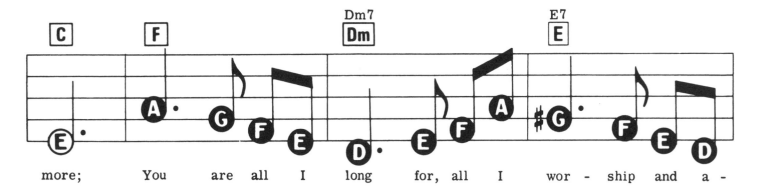

more; You are all I long for, all I wor - ship and a -

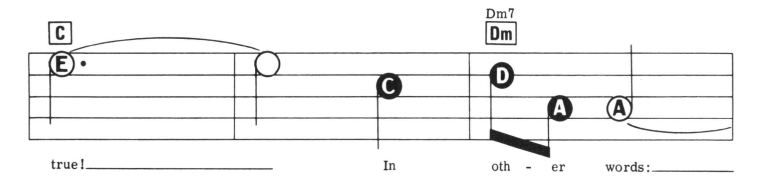

dore. In oth - er words:_____ Please be

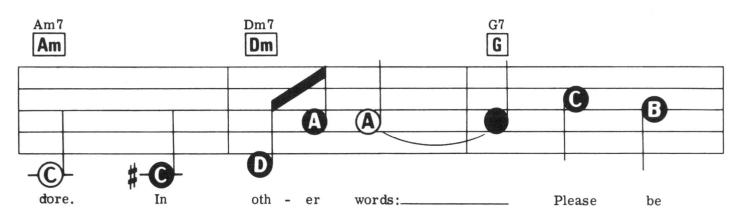

true!_____ In oth - er words:_____

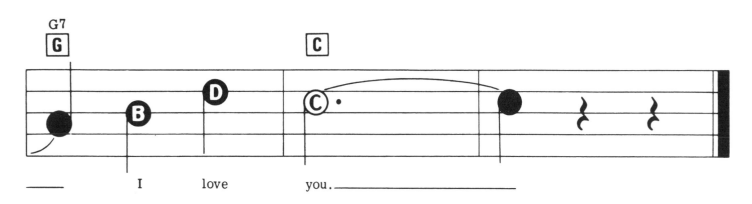

_____ I love you._____

# From a Distance

Registration 7
Rhythm: 8 Beat or Pops

Words and Music by
Julie Gold

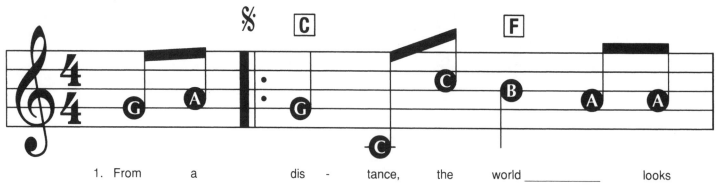

1. From a dis - tance, the world _____ looks

2., 3. *(See Additional Lyrics)*

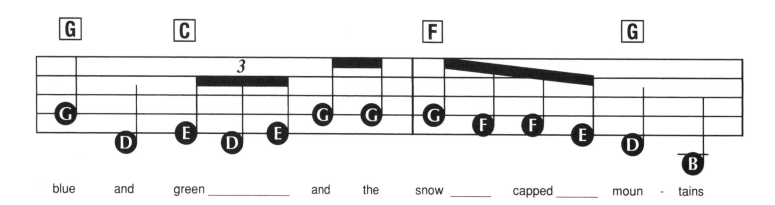

blue and green _____ and the snow _____ capped _____ moun - tains

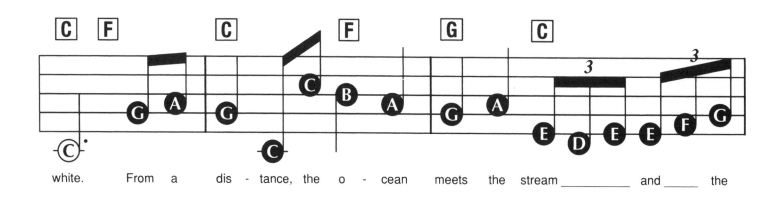

white. From a dis - tance, the o - cean meets the stream _____ and _____ the

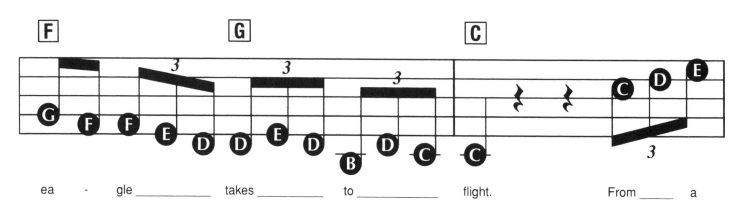

ea - gle _____ takes _____ to _____ flight. From _____ a

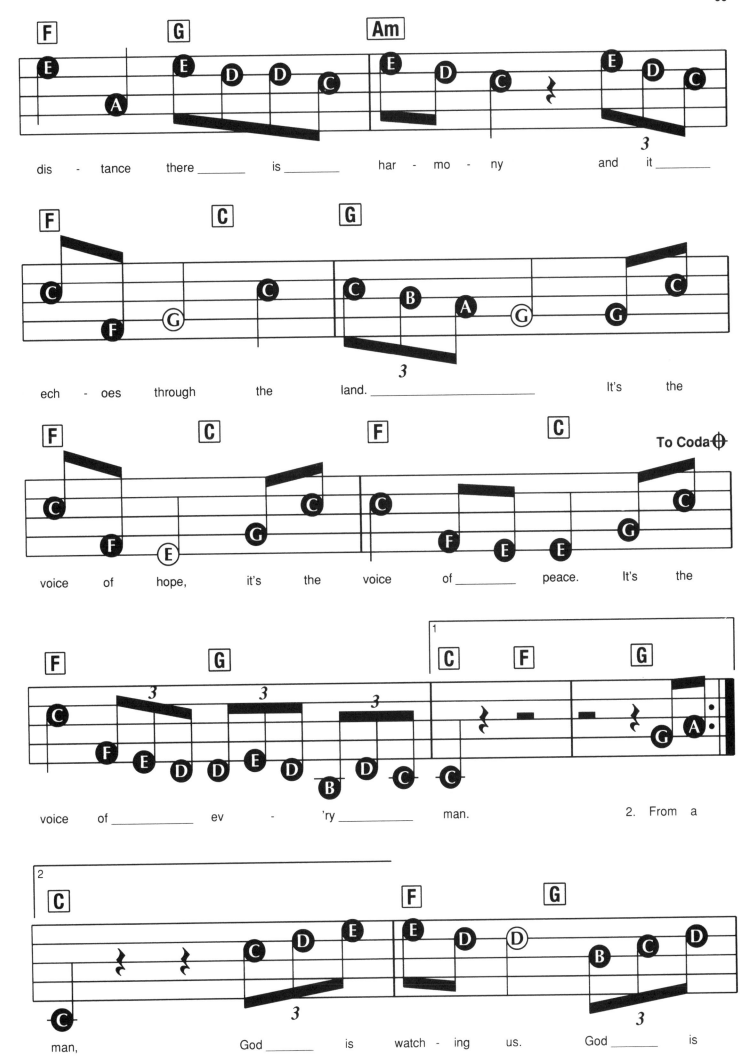

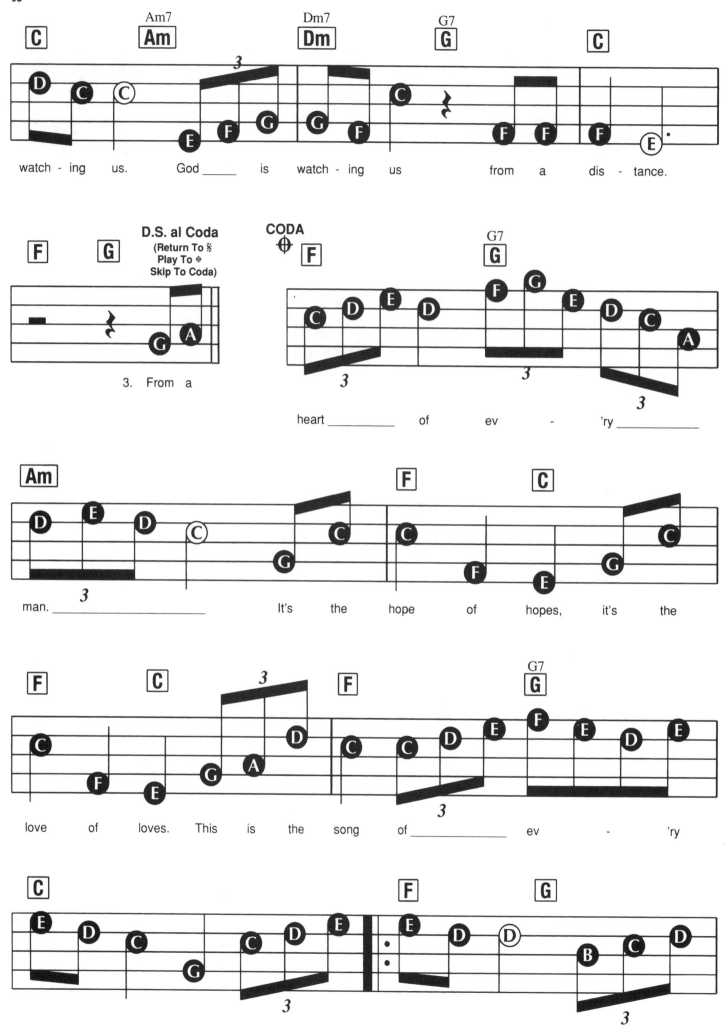

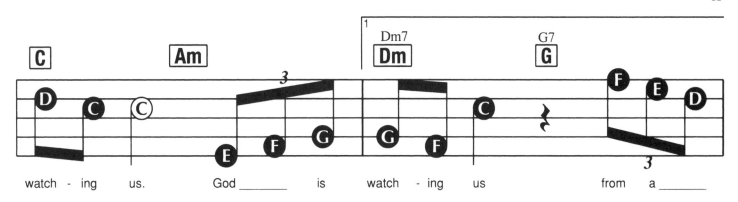

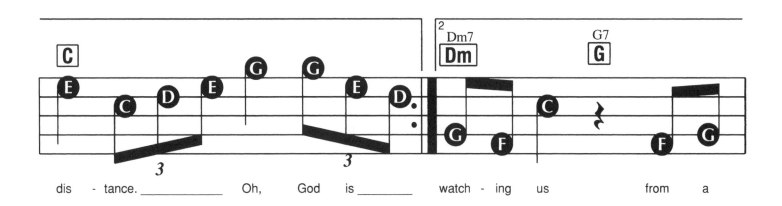

watch - ing us. God _____ is watch - ing us from a _____

dis - tance. _____ Oh, God is _____ watch - ing us from a

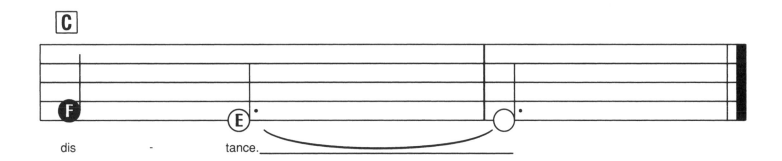

dis - tance. _____

*Additional Lyrics*

2. From a distance, we all have enough,
   And no one is in need.
   There are no guns, no bombs, no diseases,
   No hungry mouths to feed.
   From a distance, we are instruments
   Marching in a common band;
   Playing songs of hope, playing songs of peace,
   They're the songs of every man.

3. From a distance, you look like my friend
   Even though we are at war.
   From a distance I just cannot comprehend
   What all this fighting is for.
   From a distance there is harmony
   And it echos through the land.
   It's the hope of hopes, it's the love of loves.
   It's the heart of every man.

# Georgia on My Mind

Registration 4
Rhythm: Swing

Words by Stuart Gorrell
Music by Hoagy Carmichael

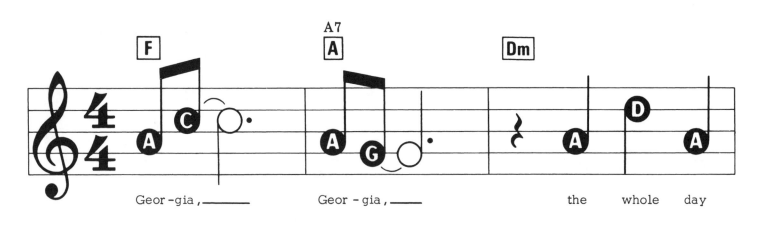

Geor-gia,_____ Geor-gia,_____ the whole day

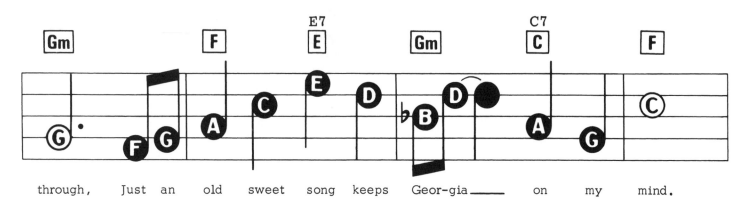

through, Just an old sweet song keeps Geor-gia_____ on my mind.

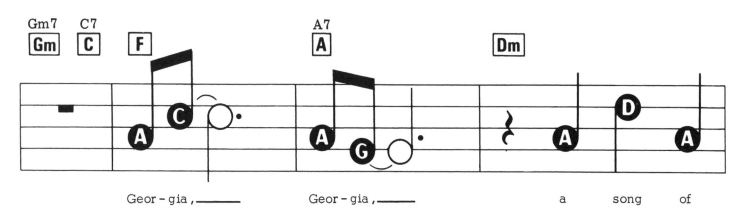

Geor-gia,_____ Geor-gia,_____ a song of

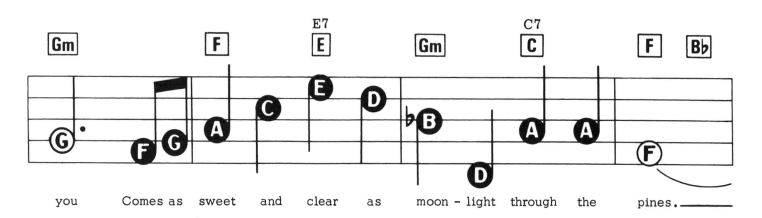

you Comes as sweet and clear as moon-light through the pines._____

43

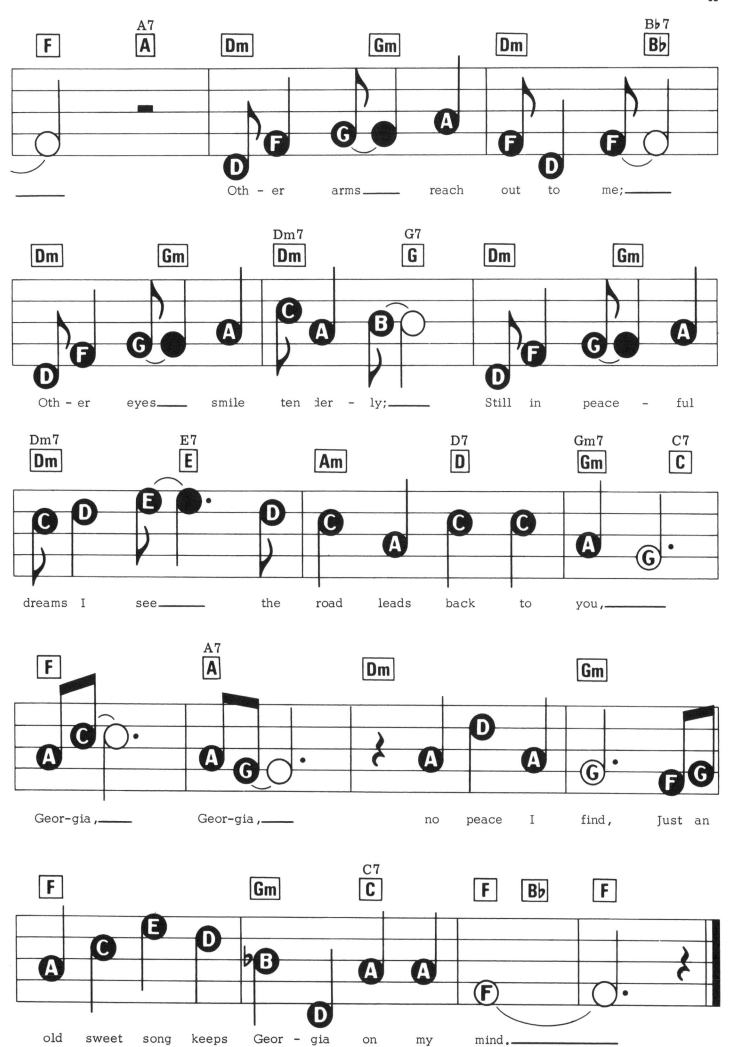

# The Girl from Ipanema
## (Garôta De Ipanema)

Registration 4
Rhythm: Latin or Bossa Nova

Music by Antonio Carlos Jobim
English Words by Norman Gimbel
Original Words by Vinicius de Moraes

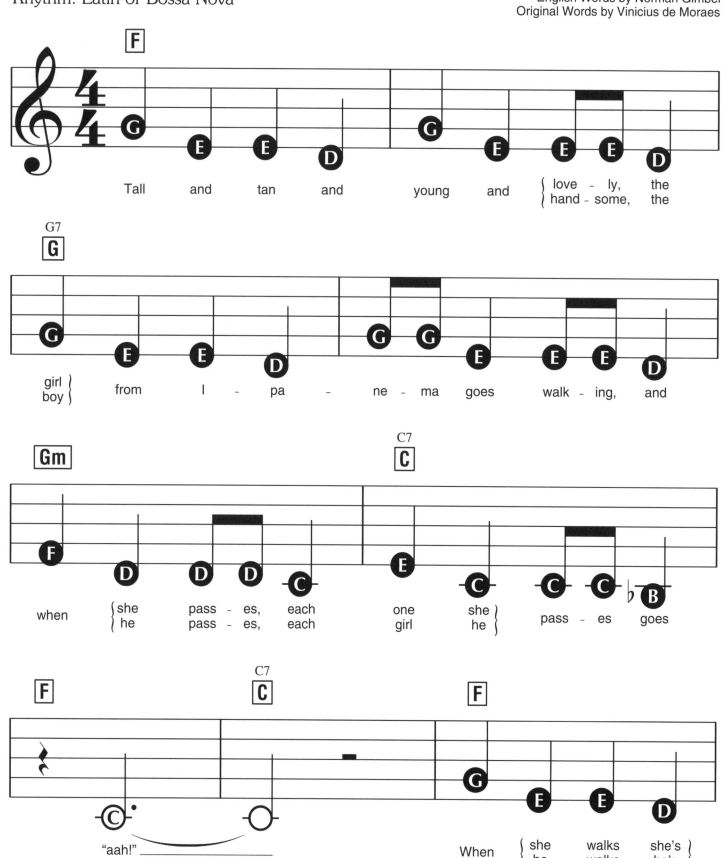

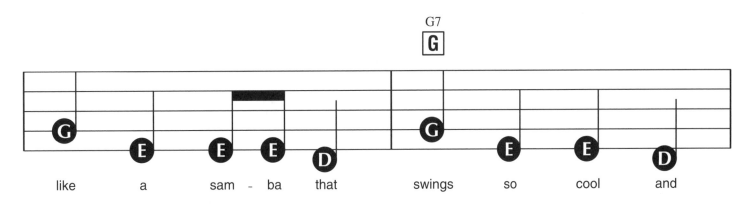

like a sam - ba that swings so cool and

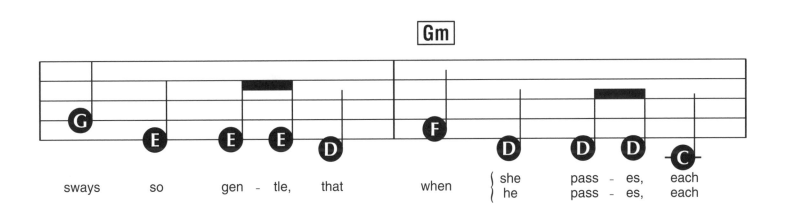

sways so gen - tle, that when { she / he } pass - es, { each / each }

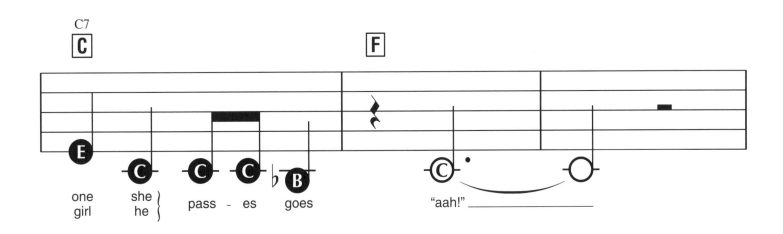

{ one girl / he } she { pass - es goes "aah!"

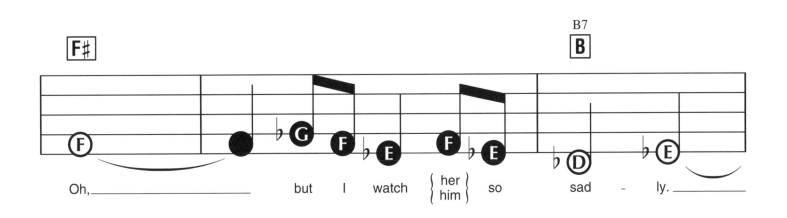

Oh, but I watch { her / him } so sad - ly.

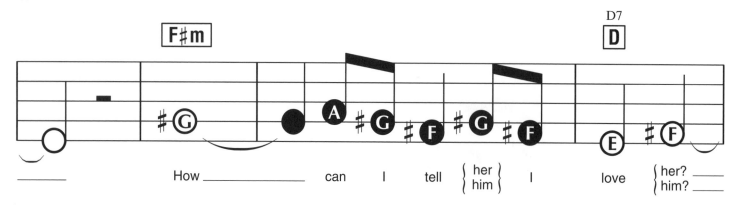

How _____ can I tell { her / him } I love { her? / him? } _____

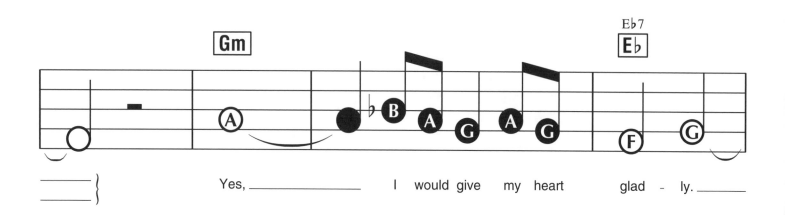

_____ } Yes, _____ I would give my heart glad - ly. _____

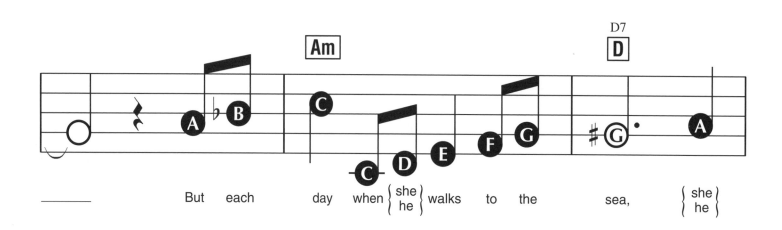

_____ But each day when { she / he } walks to the sea, { she / he }

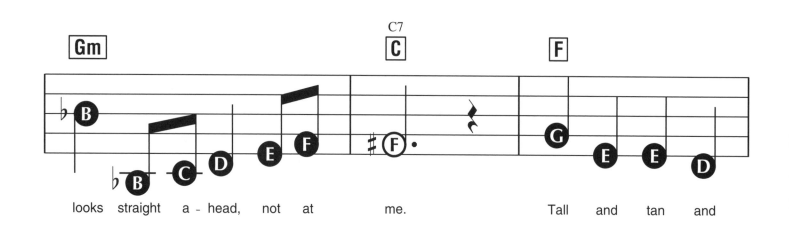

looks straight a - head, not at me. Tall and tan and

47

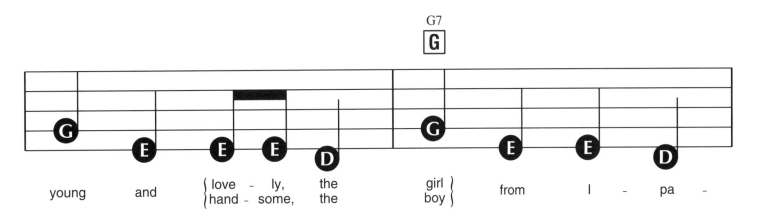

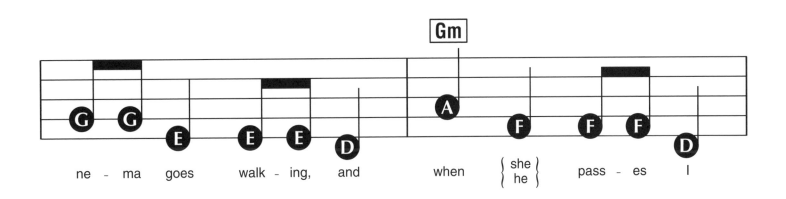

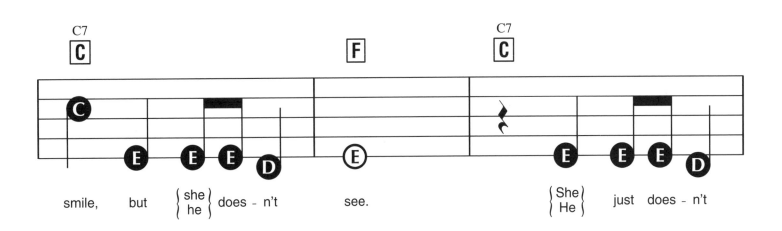

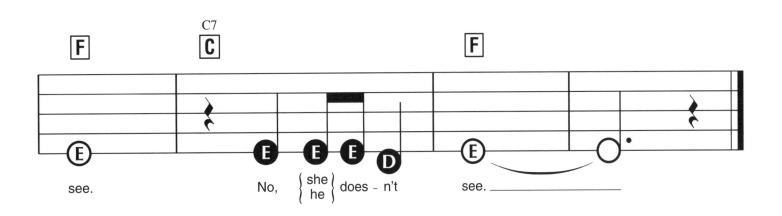

# Here's That Rainy Day
## from CARNIVAL IN FLANDERS

Registration 2
Rhythm: Ballad or Slow Rock

Words by Johnny Burke
Music by Jimmy Van Heusen

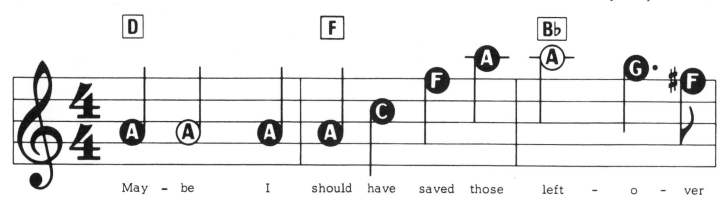

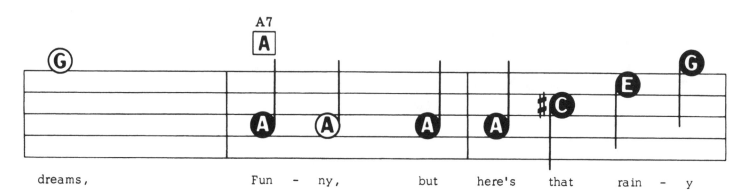

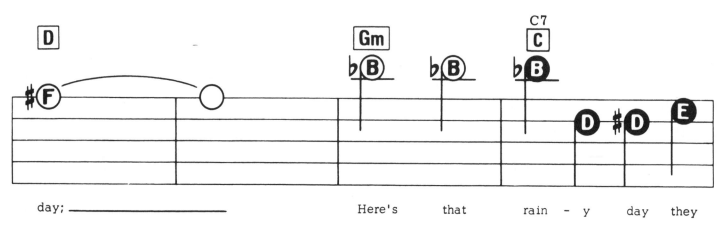

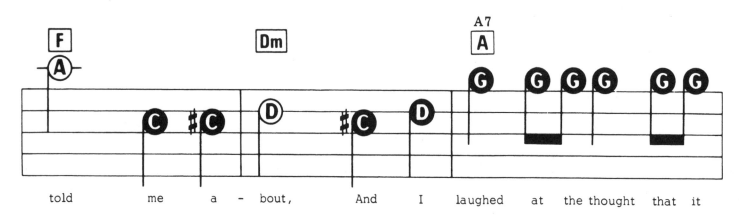

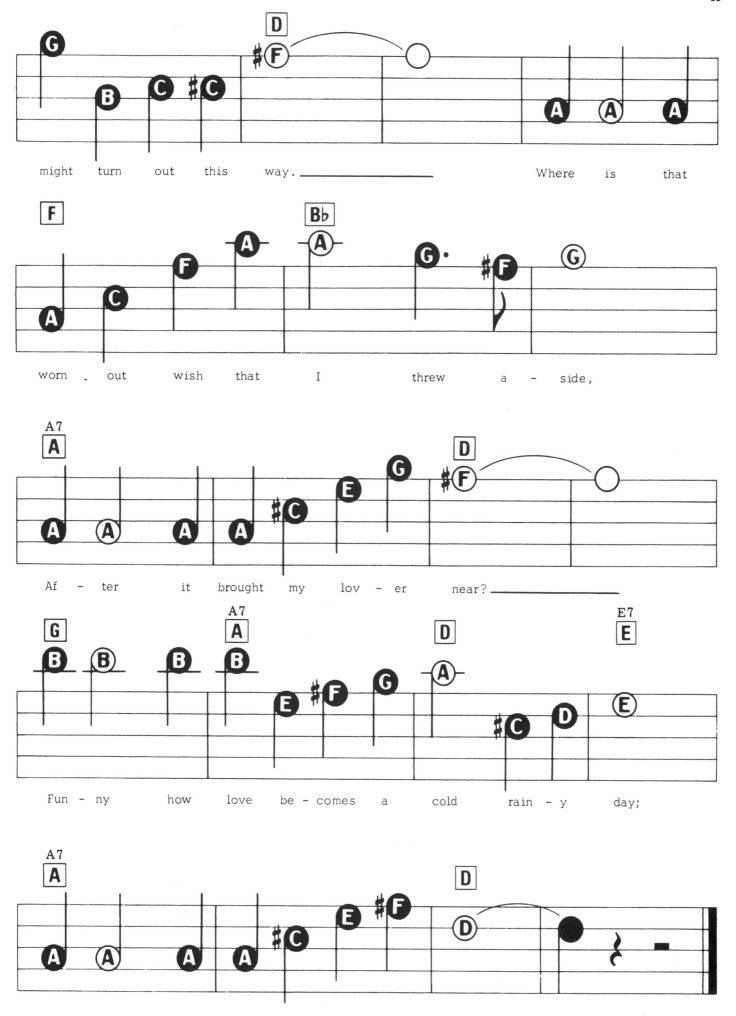

# How Deep Is the Ocean

## (How High Is the Sky)

Registration 4
Rhythm: Fox Trot or Swing

Words and Music by
Irving Berlin

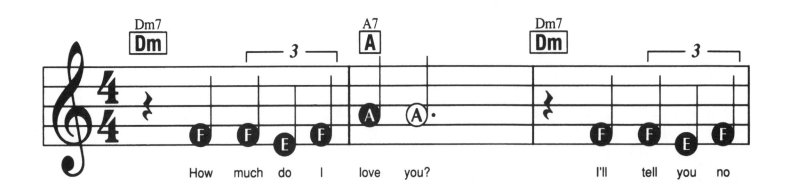

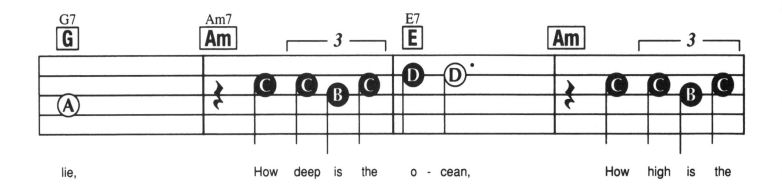

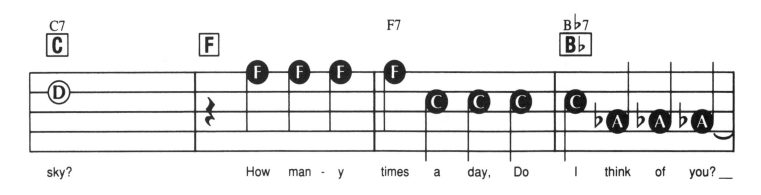

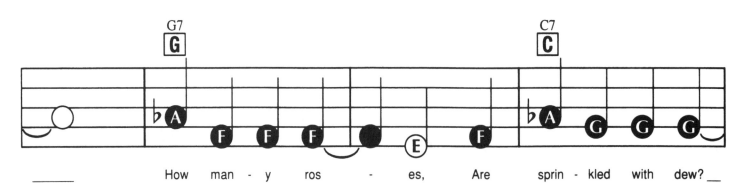

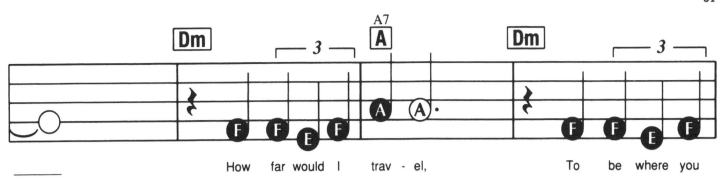

How far would I trav - el, To be where you

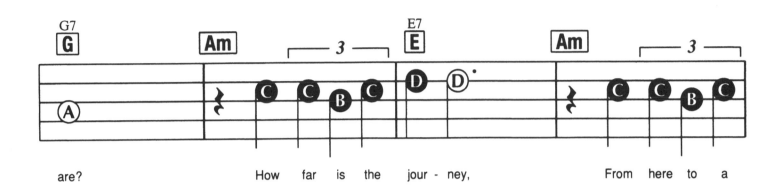

are? How far is the jour - ney, From here to a

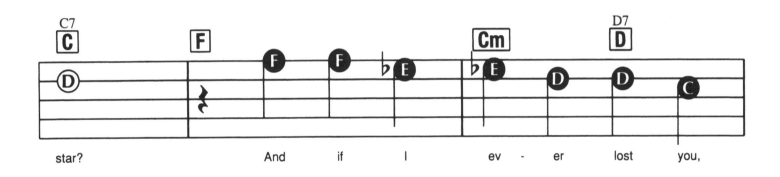

star? And if I ev - er lost you,

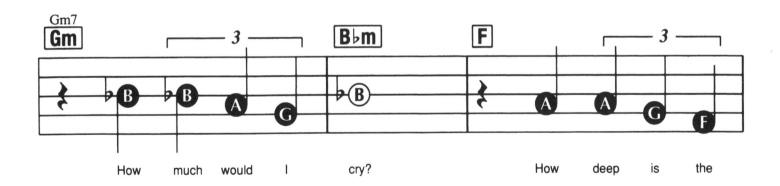

How much would I cry? How deep is the

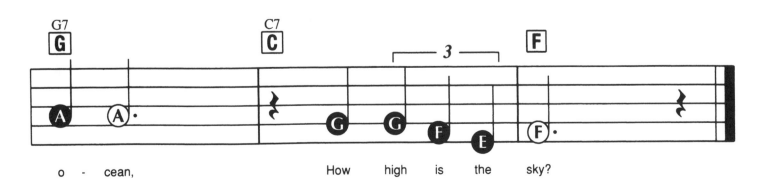

o - cean, How high is the sky?

# I Left My Heart in San Francisco

Registration 9
Rhythm: Fox Trot

Words by Douglass Cross
Music by George Cory

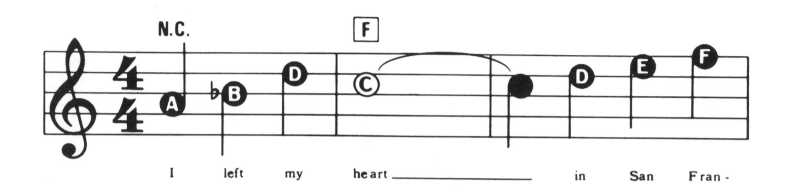

I left my heart _____ in San Fran-

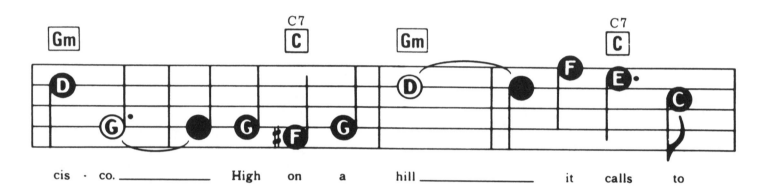

cis · co. _____ High on a hill _____ it calls to

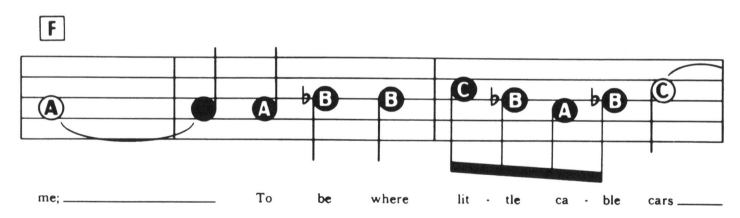

me; _____ To be where lit · tle ca · ble cars _____

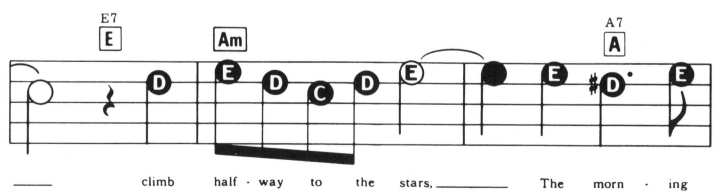

_____ climb half · way to the stars, _____ The morn · ing

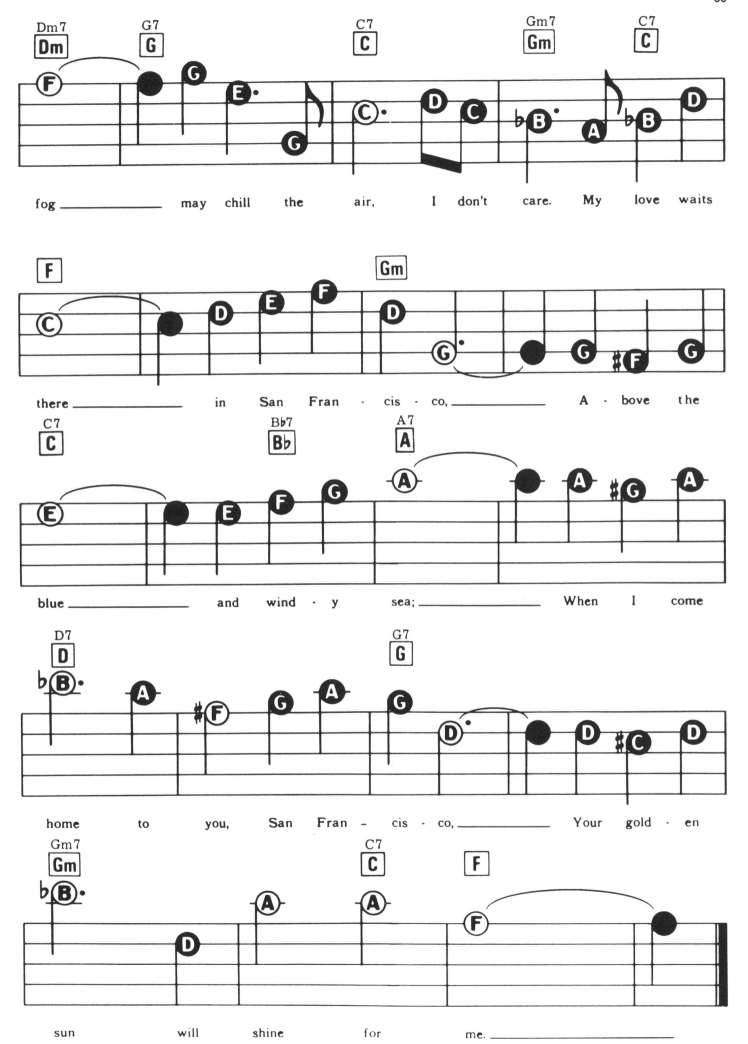

# I'll Be Seeing You

## from RIGHT THIS WAY

Registration 5
Rhythm: Swing

Lyric by Irving Kahal
Music by Sammy Fain

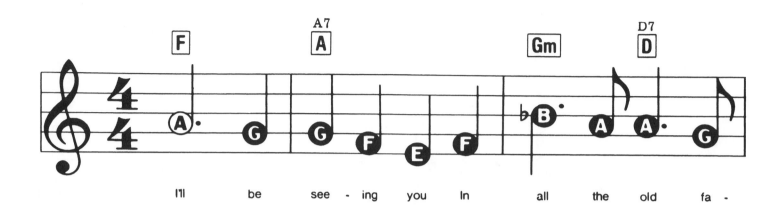

I'll be see - ing you In all the old fa -

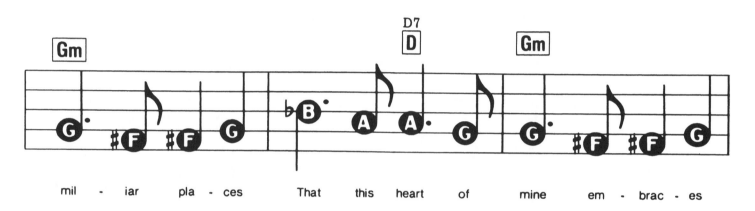

mil - iar pla - ces That this heart of mine em - brac - es

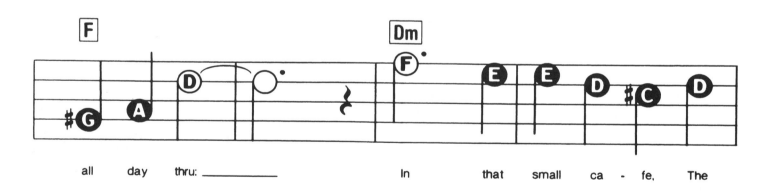

all day thru: _____ In that small ca - fe, The

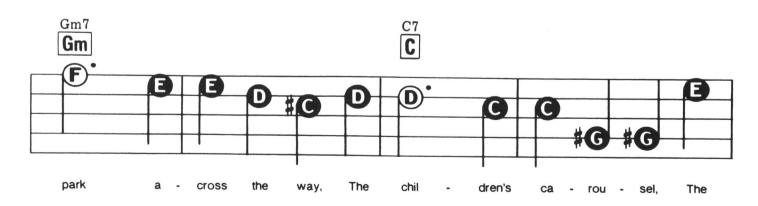

park a - cross the way, The chil - dren's ca - rou - sel, The

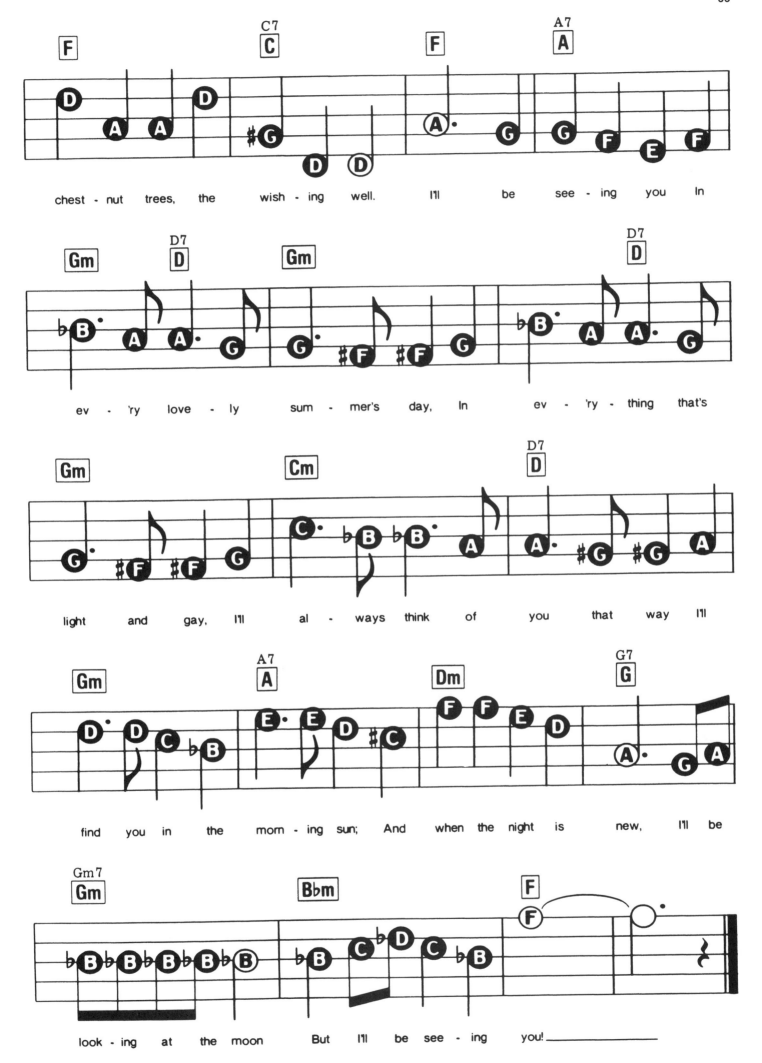

# Imagine

Registration 8
Rhythm: Rock or Slow Rock

Words and Music by
John Lennon

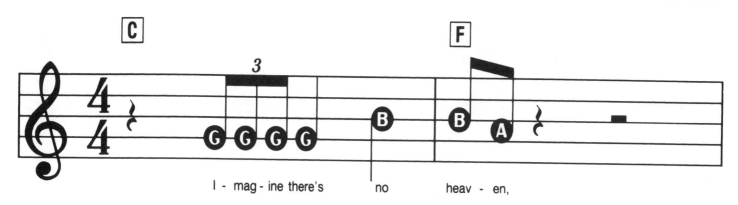

I - mag - ine there's    no    heav - en,

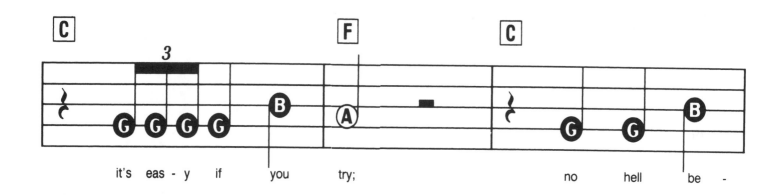

it's eas - y   if   you   try;         no   hell   be -

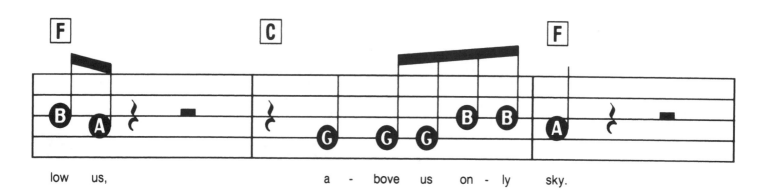

low us,              a - bove us on - ly sky.

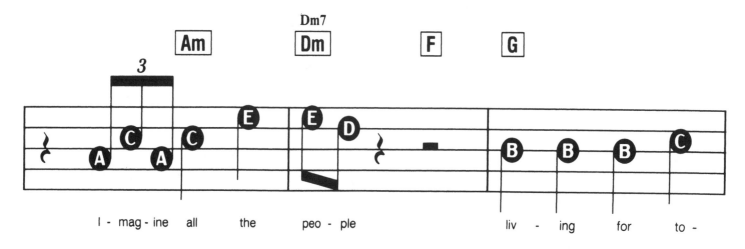

I - mag - ine all   the   peo - ple         liv - ing for to -

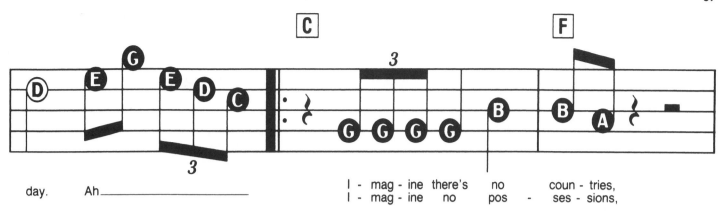

day.  Ah _____

I - mag - ine there's  no  coun - tries,
I - mag - ine  no  pos - ses - sions,

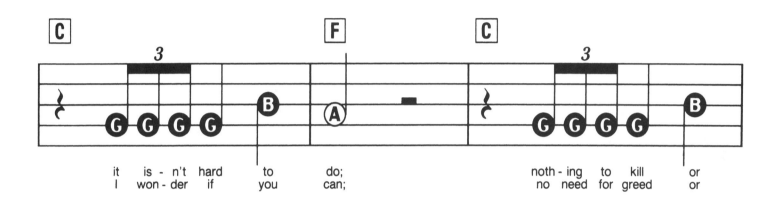

it  is - n't  hard  to  do;
I  won - der  if  you  can;

noth - ing  to  kill  or
no  need  for  greed  or

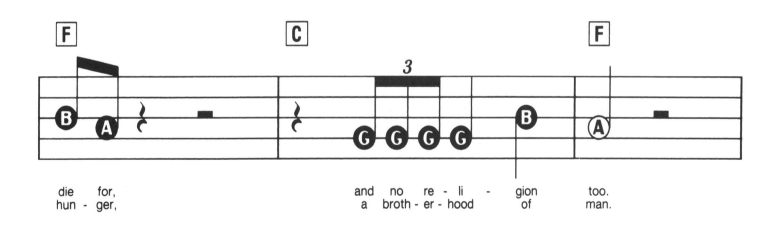

die  for,
hun - ger,

and  no  re - li - gion  too.
a  broth - er - hood  of  man.

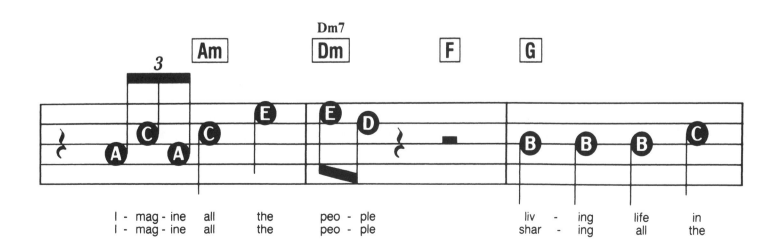

I - mag - ine  all  the  peo - ple
I - mag - ine  all  the  peo - ple

liv - ing  life  in
shar - ing  all  in  the

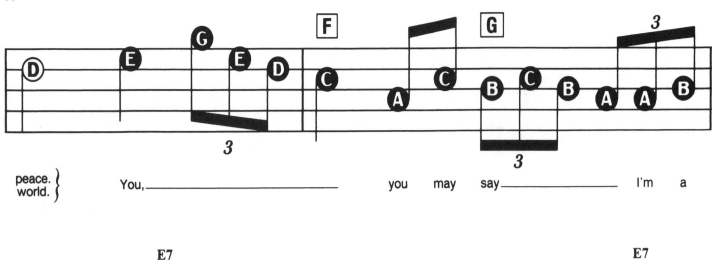

peace.
world.

You,_____ you may say_____ I'm a

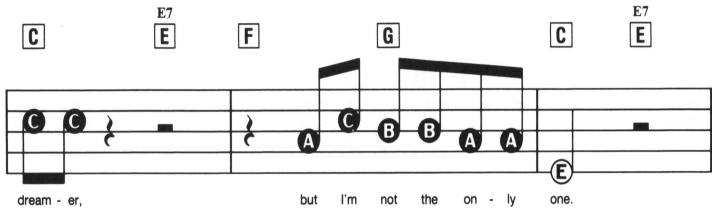

dream - er,

but I'm not the on - ly one.

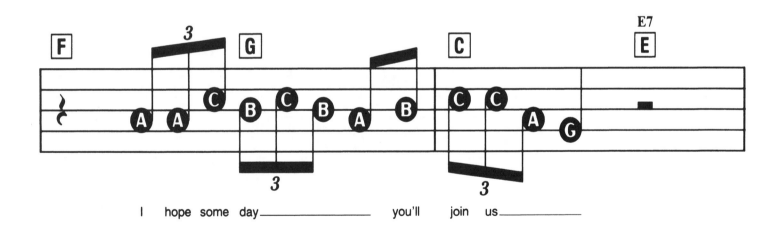

I hope some day_____ you'll join us_____

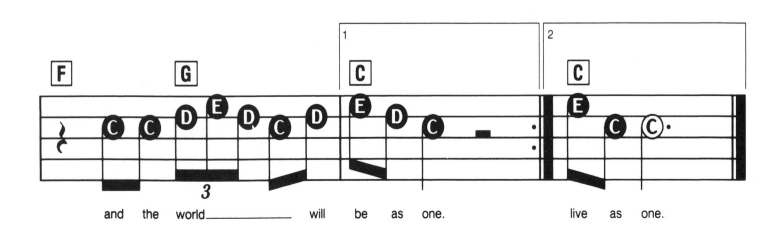

and the world_____ will be as one.

live as one.

# My Way

English Words by Paul Anka
Original French Words by Gilles Thibault
Music by Jacques Revaux and Claude Francois

Registration 5
Rhythm: Ballad or Rock

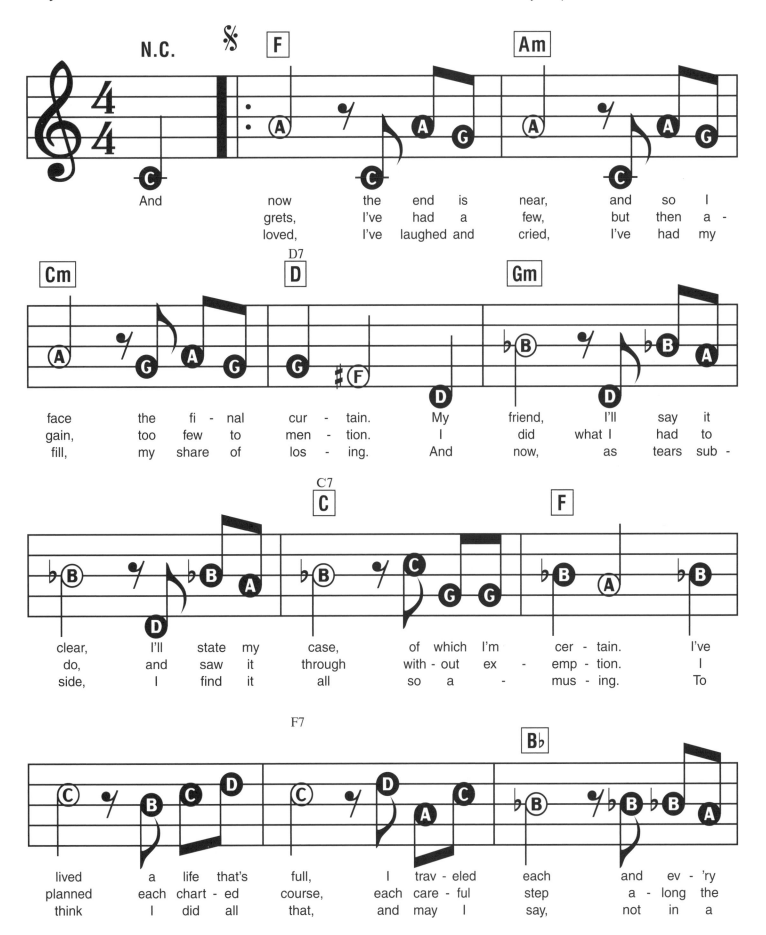

high - way,     and     more,     much   more   than   this,     I     did     it
by - way,     and     more,     much   much   more   than   this,     I     did     it
shy   way,     "Oh,     no,     oh     no,     not     me,     I     did     it

To Coda

my                          way.           Re -          way.     Yes,   there   were

times,     I'm   sure   you   knew,     when     I     bit     off     more   than   I   could

chew,     but through   it     all,     when   there   was     doubt,     I     ate   it

up     and   spit   it     out.     I   faced   it     all     and   I   stood

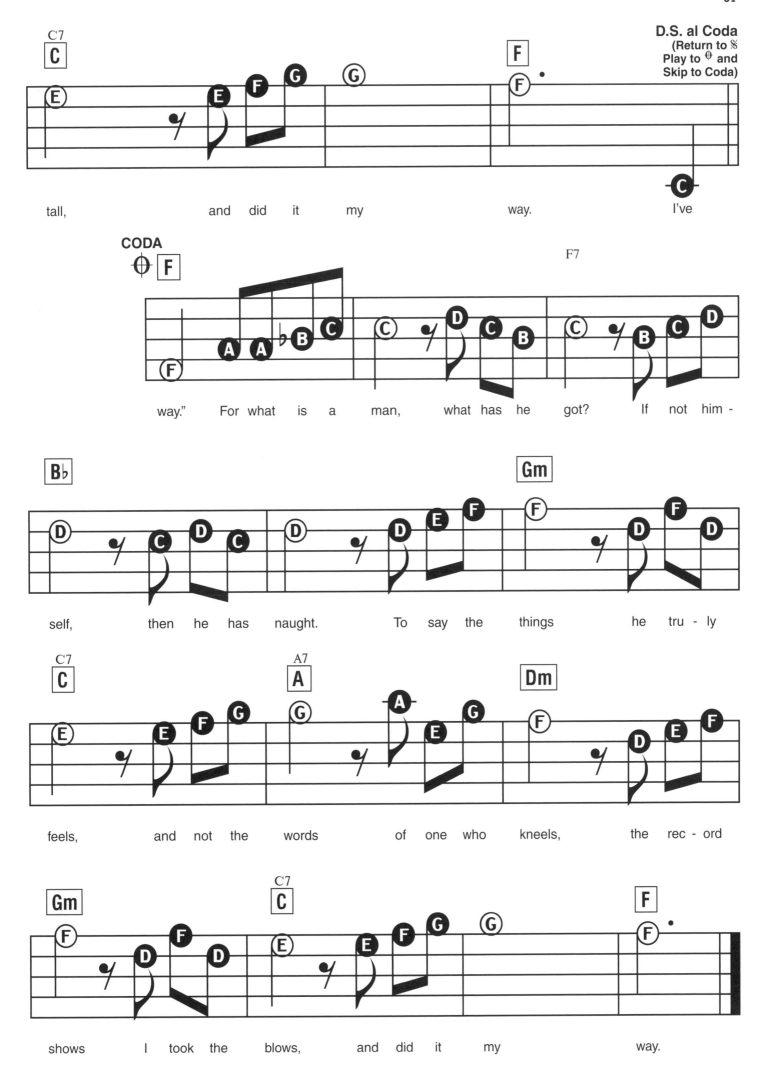

D.S. al Coda
(Return to 𝄋
Play to ⊕ and
Skip to Coda)

# Isn't It Romantic?

**from the Paramount Picture LOVE ME TONIGHT**

Registration 2
Rhythm: Swing or Big Band

Words by Lorenz Hart
Music by Richard Rodgers

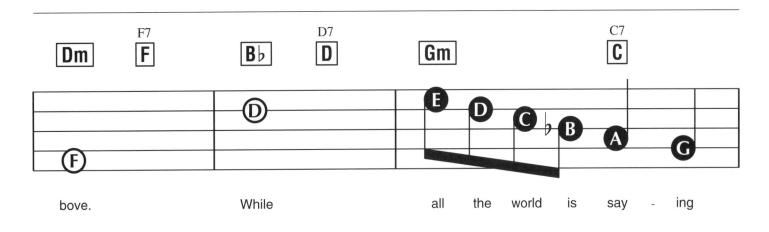

bove.    While    all  the  world  is  say - ing

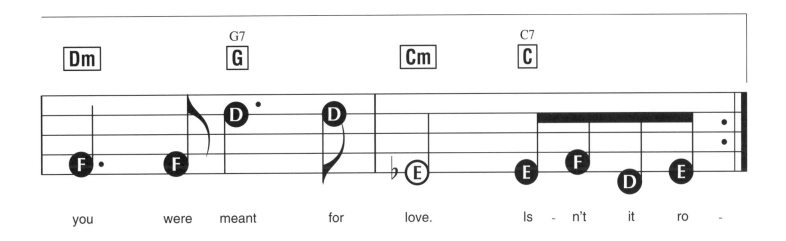

you    were   meant    for    love.    Is - n't  it  ro -

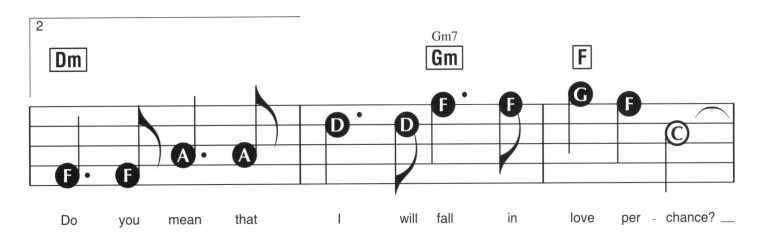

Do  you  mean  that    I  will  fall  in  love  per - chance? ___

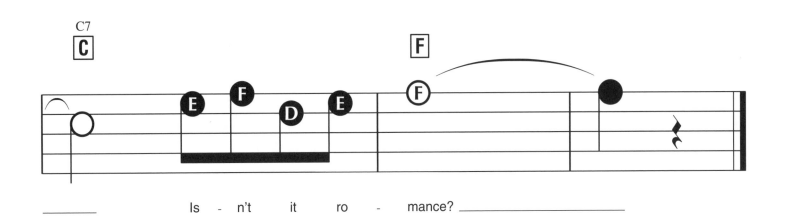

___    Is - n't  it  ro - mance? _____

# It Might As Well Be Spring
## from STATE FAIR

Registration 3
Rhythm: Ballad

Lyrics by Oscar Hammerstein II
Music by Richard Rodgers

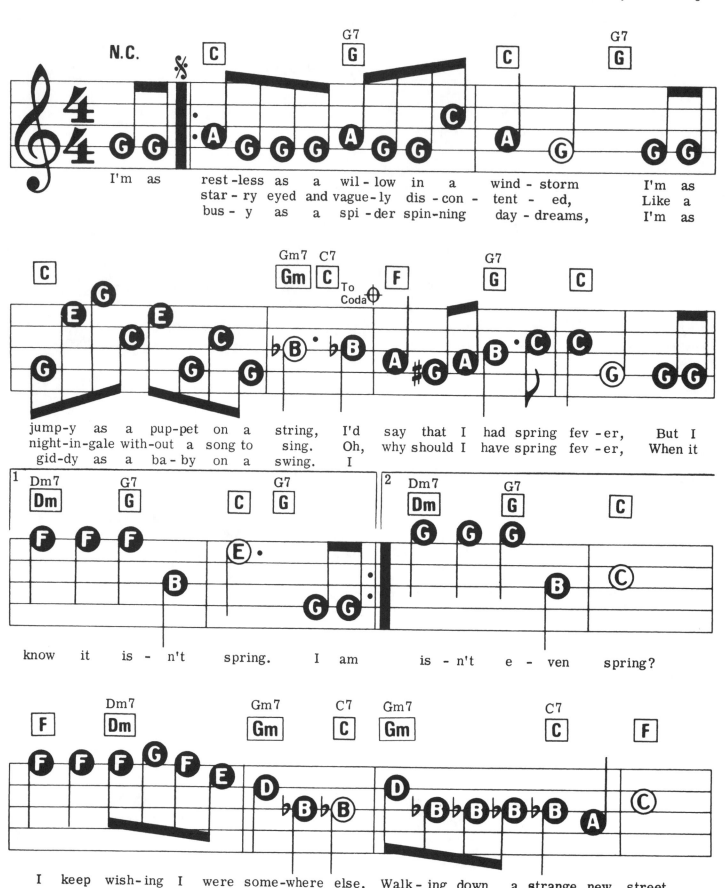

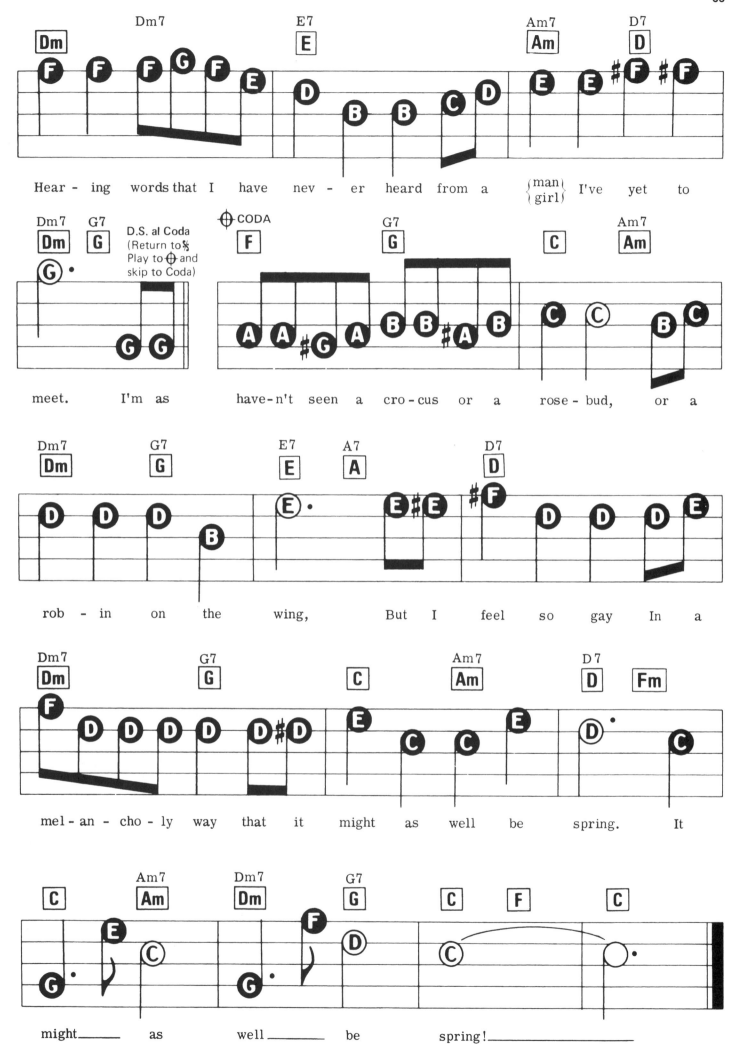

# Just the Way You Are

Registration 4
Rhythm: Rock or Jazz Rock

Words and Music by
Billy Joel

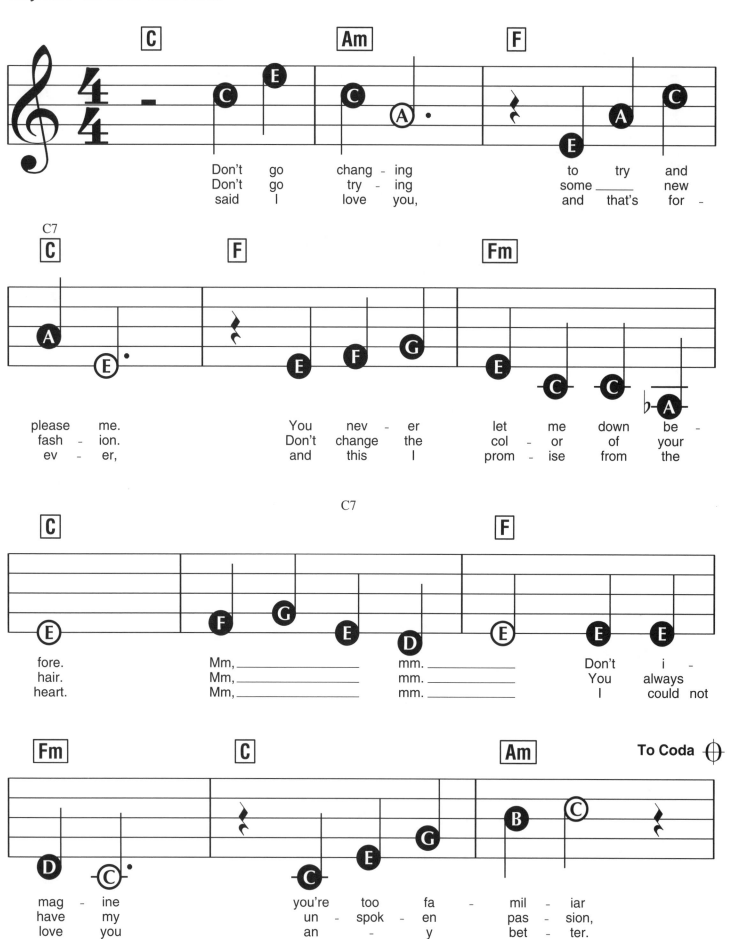

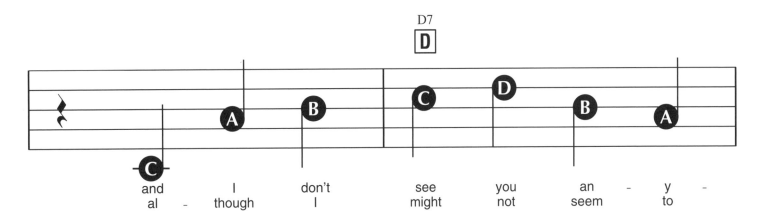

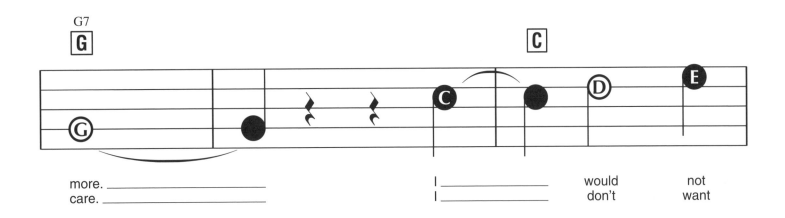

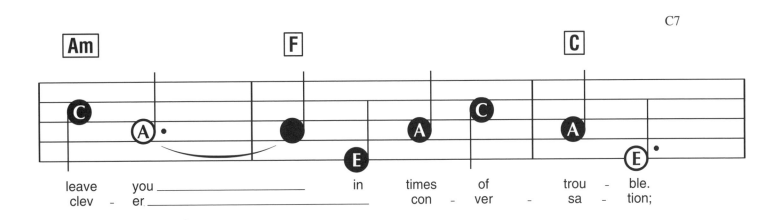

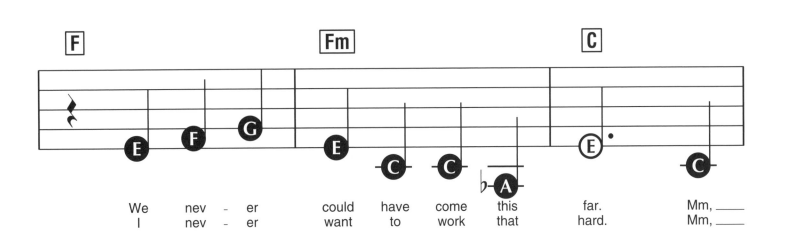

68

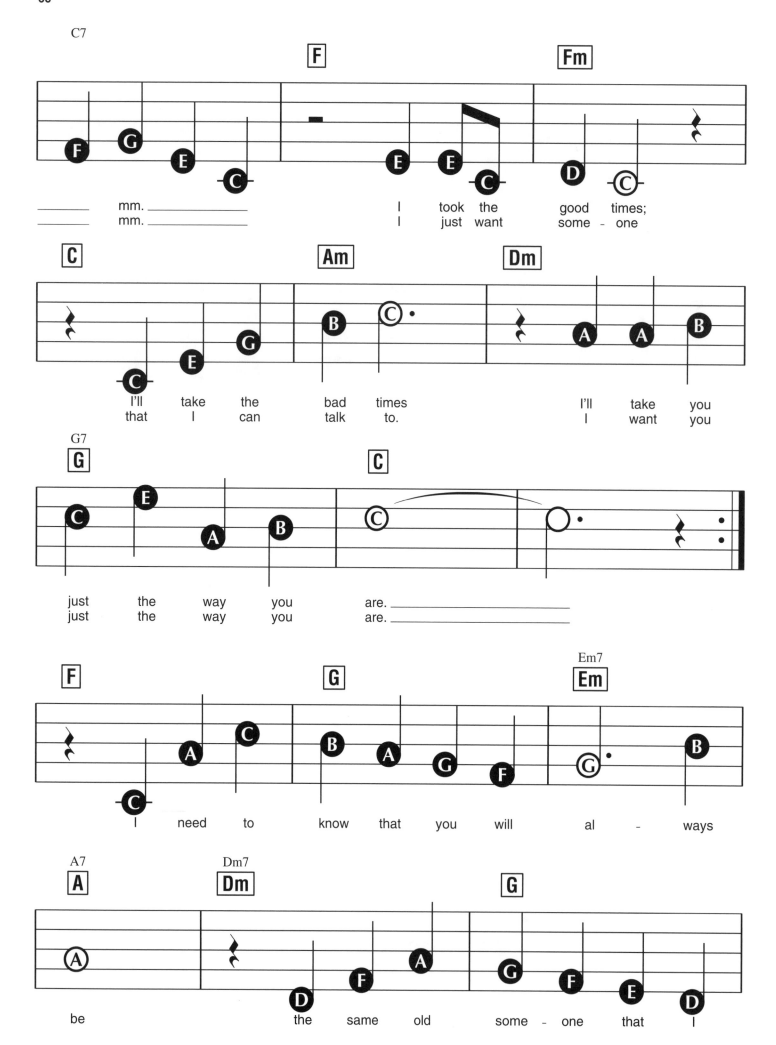

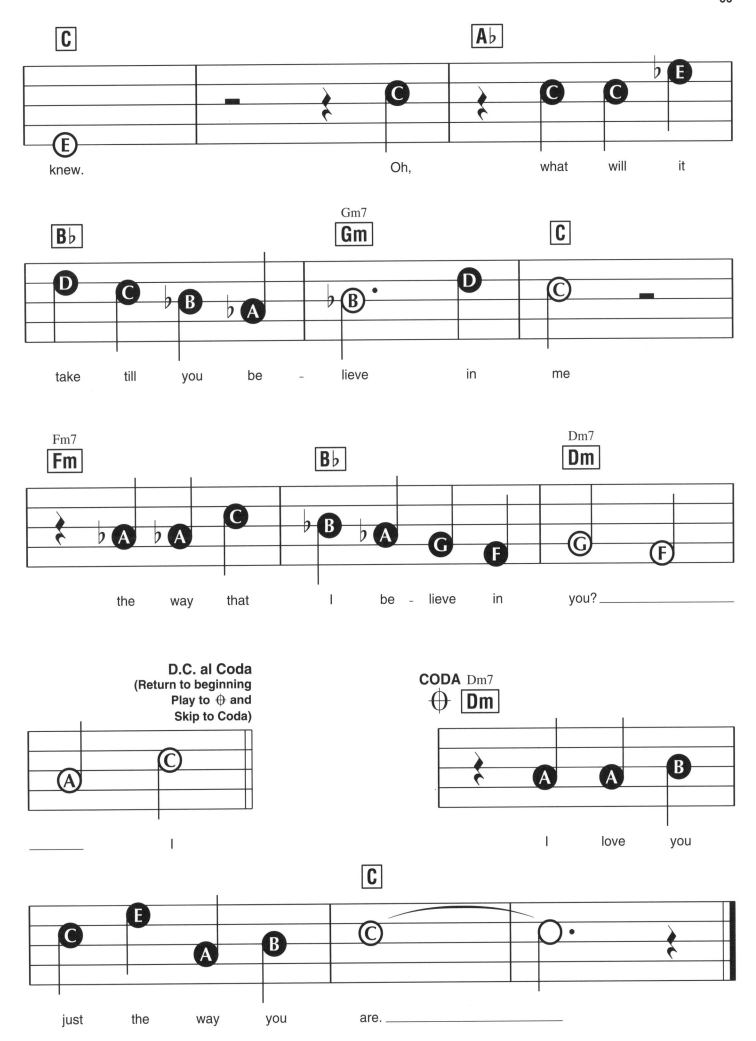

# Killing Me Softly with His Song

Registration 2
Rhythm: Rock

Words by Norman Gimbel
Music by Charles Fox

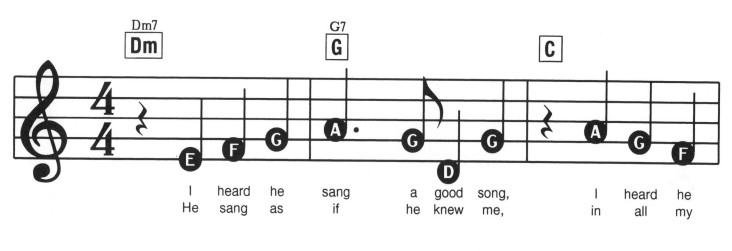

I heard he sang a good song, I heard he
He sang as if he knew me, in all my

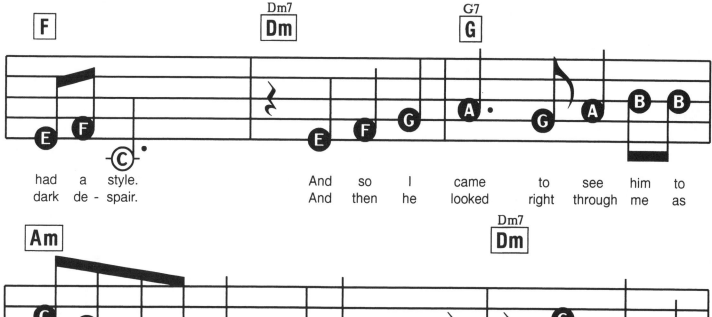

had a style.
dark de-spair.
And so I came to see him to
And then he came looked right through me as

lis - ten for a while. _____
if I was - n't there. _____

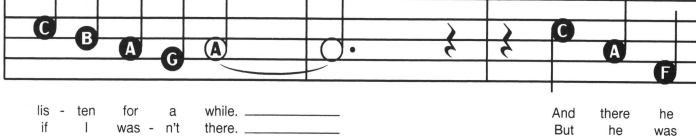

And there he
But he was

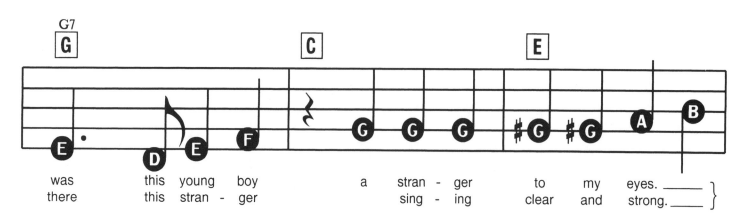

was this young boy
there this stran - ger
a stran - ger
sing - ing
to my eyes. _____
clear and strong. _____

# The Lady Is a Tramp
## from BABES IN ARMS
## from WORDS AND MUSIC

Registration 7
Rhythm: Fox Trot or Swing

Words by Lorenz Hart
Music by Richard Rodgers

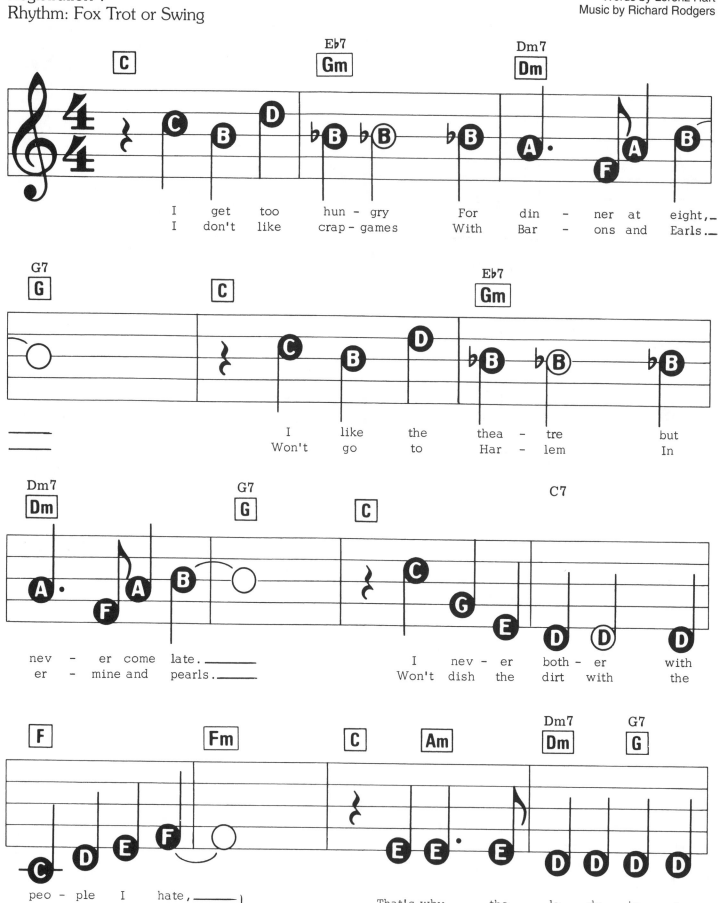

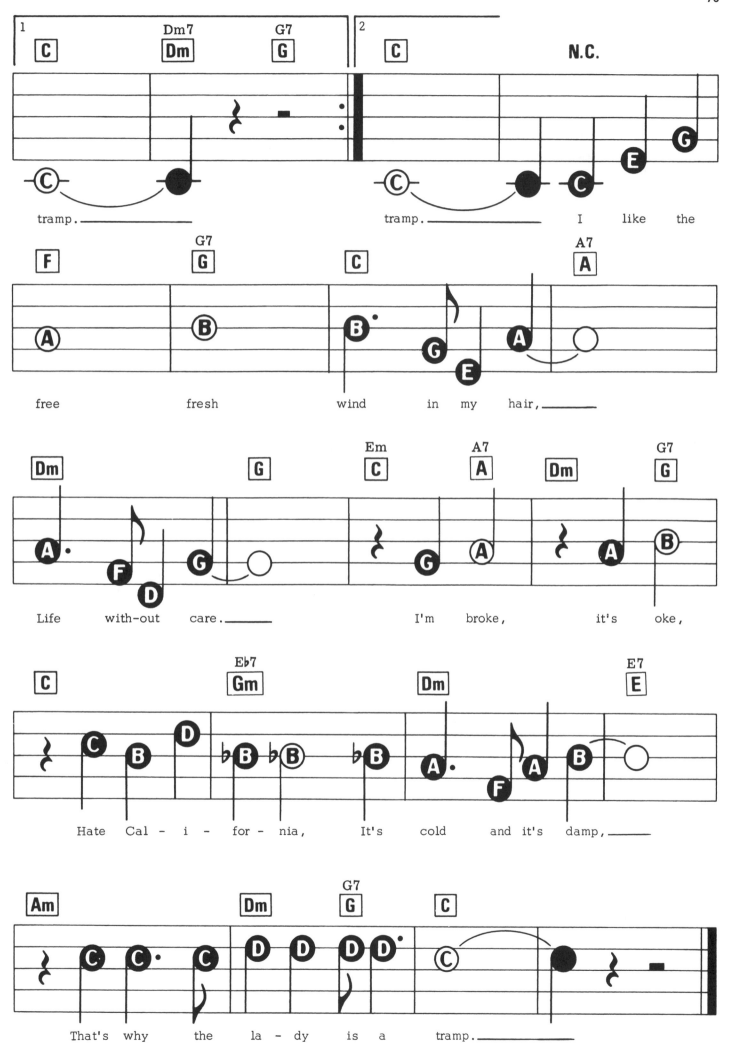

# Let It Be

Registration 3
Rhythm: Rock

Words and Music by John Lennon
and Paul McCartney

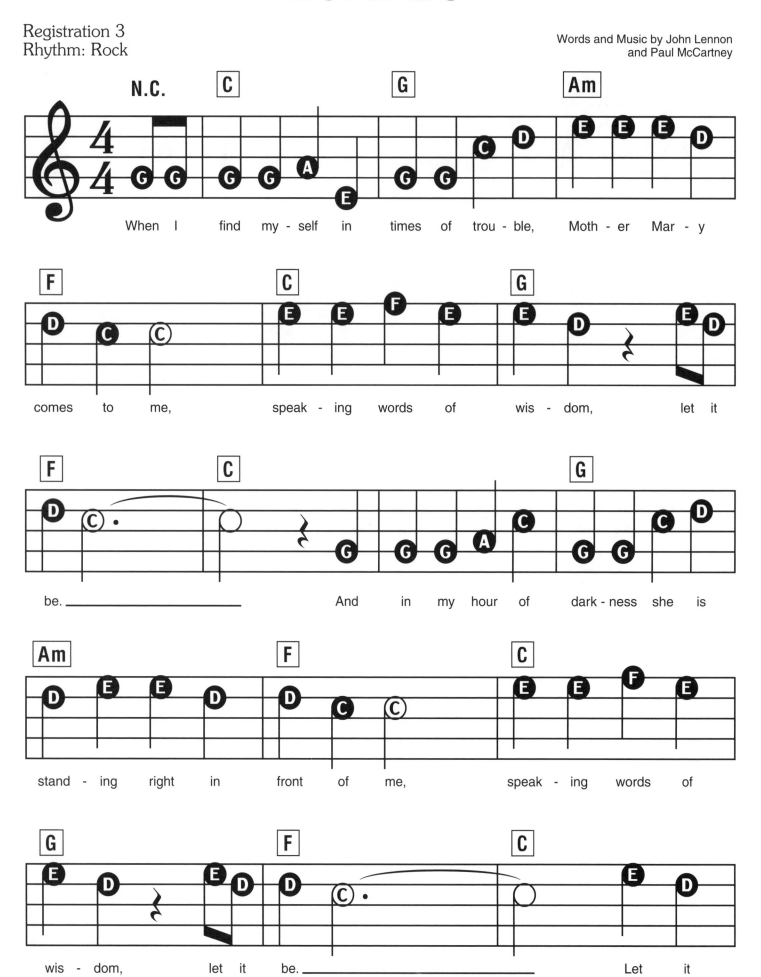

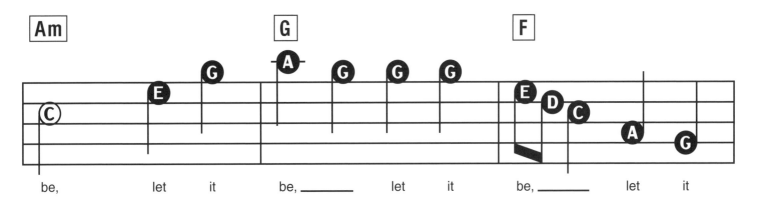

be,     let    it     be, _____ let    it     be, _____ let    it

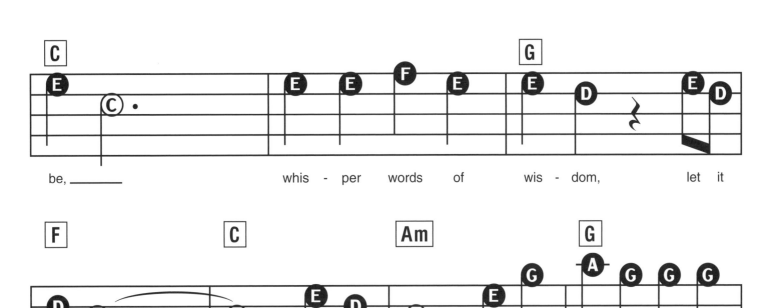

be, _____       whis - per words of    wis - dom,     let it

be. _____       Let   it    be,    let   it    be, _____ let   it

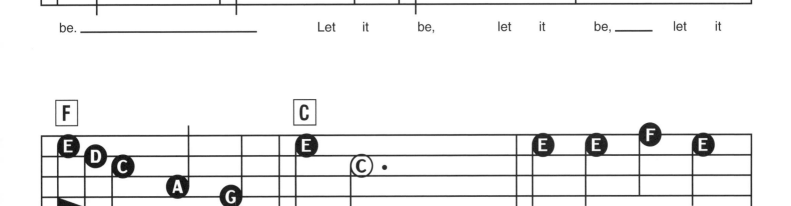

be, _____   let    it     be, _____       whis - per words of

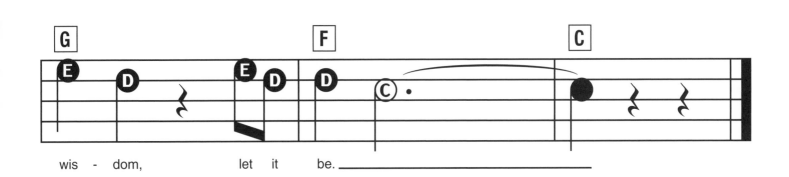

wis - dom,      let   it     be. _____

# Long Ago
## (And Far Away)
### from COVER GIRL

Registration 3
Rhythm: Ballad or Swing

Words by Ira Gershwin
Music by Jerome Kern

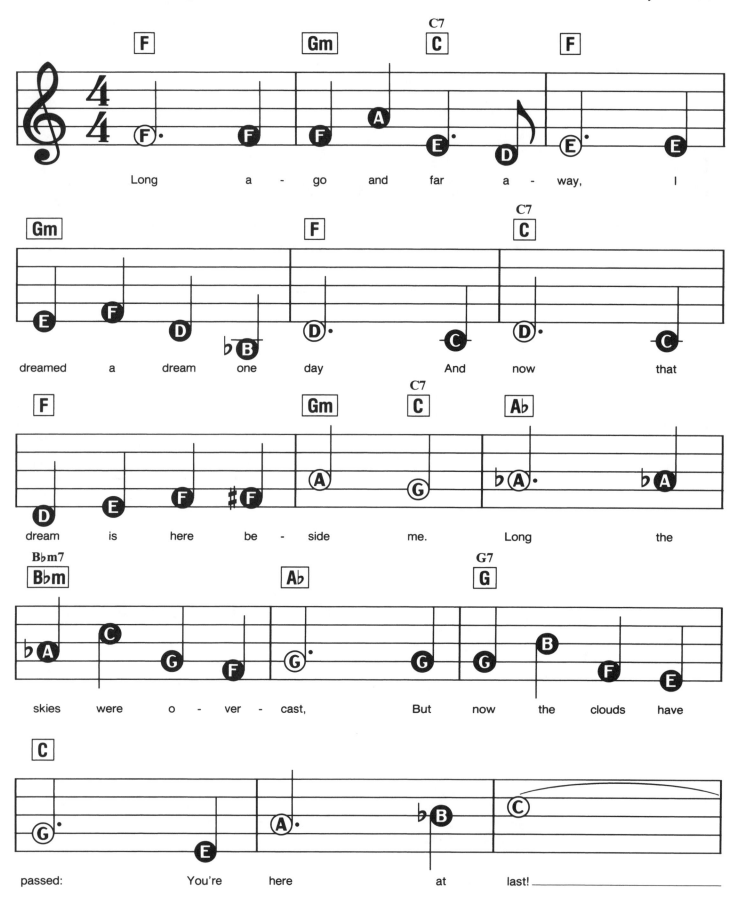

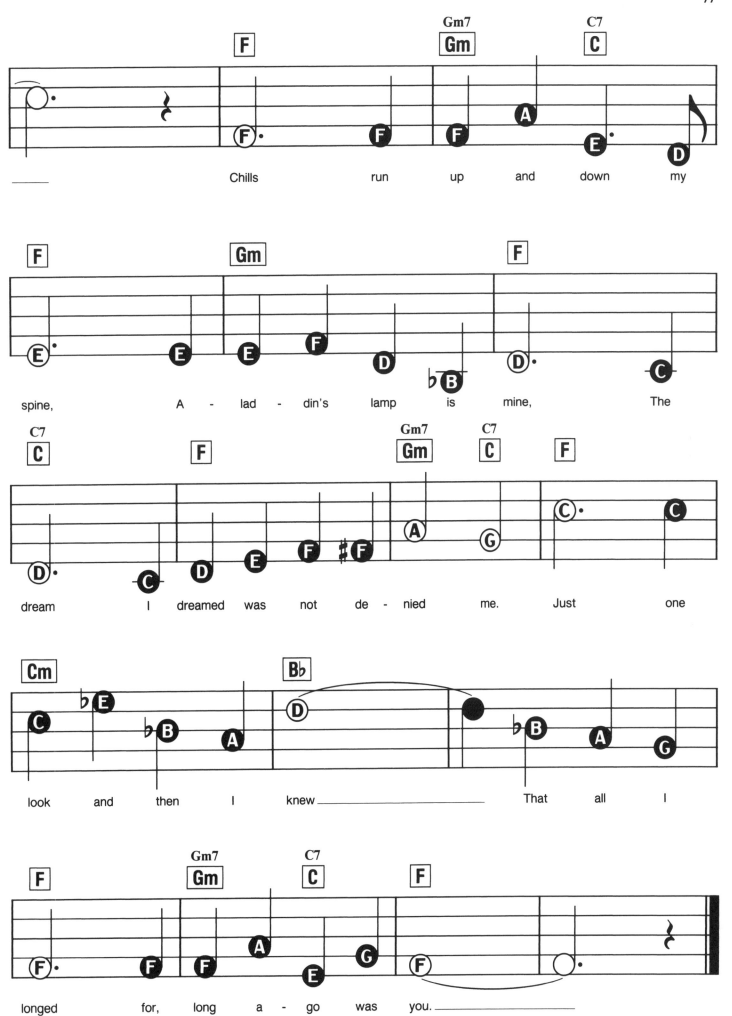

# Love Me Tender
## from LOVE ME TENDER

Registration 9
Rhythm: Slow Rock or Rock

Words and Music by Elvis Presley
and Vera Matson

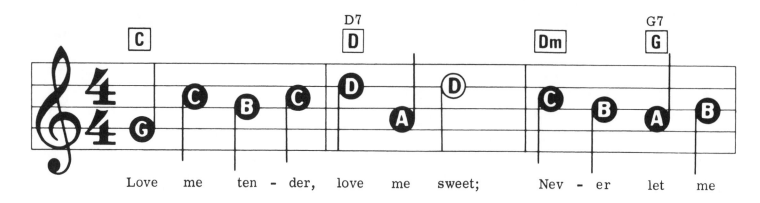

Love me ten - der, love me sweet; Nev - er let me

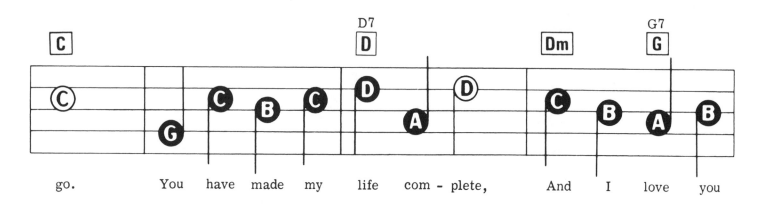

go. You have made my life com - plete, And I love you

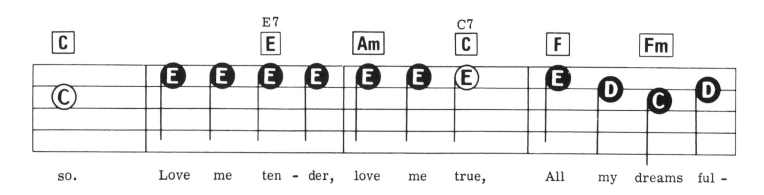

so. Love me ten - der, love me true, All my dreams ful -

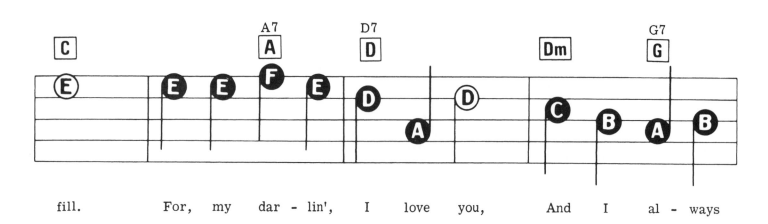

fill. For, my dar - lin', I love you, And I al - ways

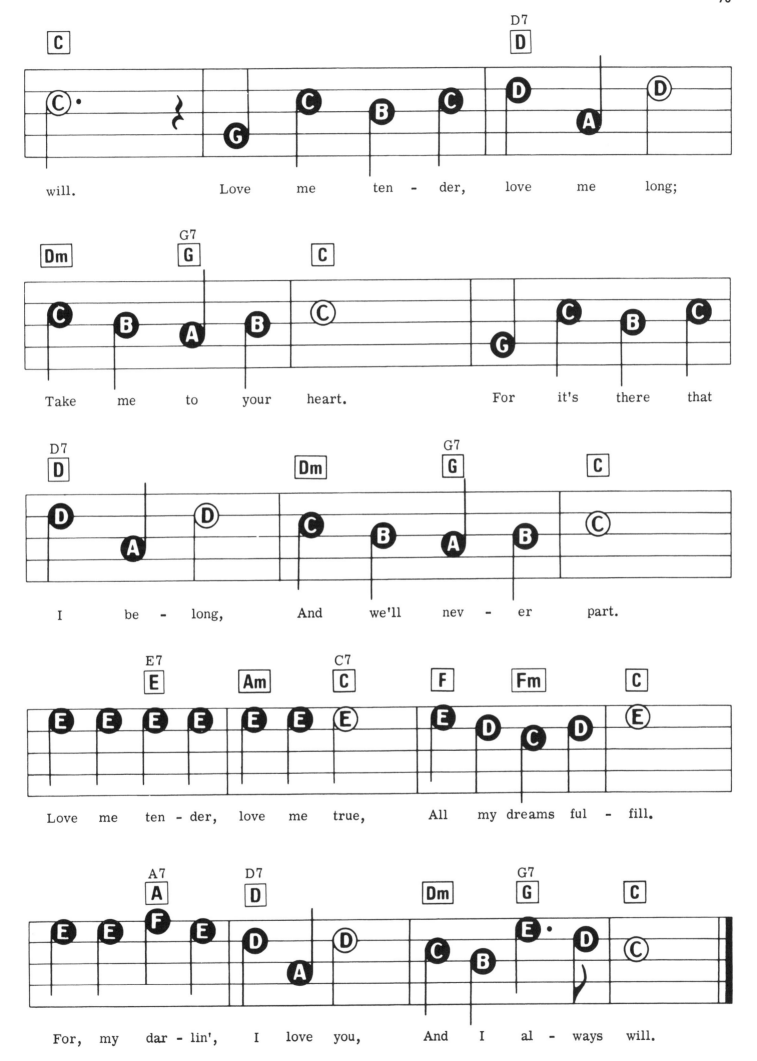

# Memory
## from CATS

Registration 3
Rhythm: 6/8 March

Music by Andrew Lloyd Webber
Text by Trevor Nunn after T.S. Eliot

81

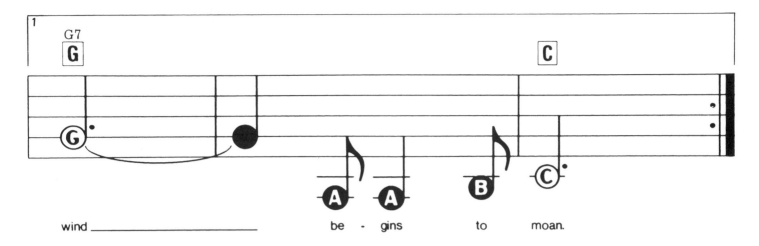

wind _____ be - gins to moan.

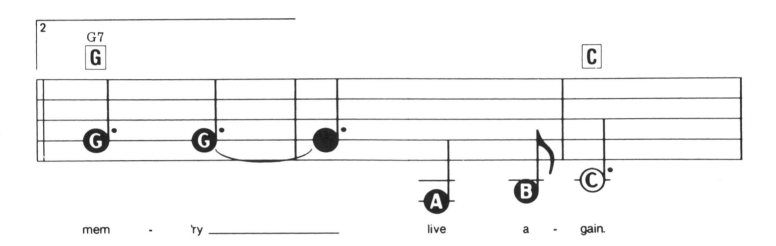

mem - 'ry _____ live a - gain.

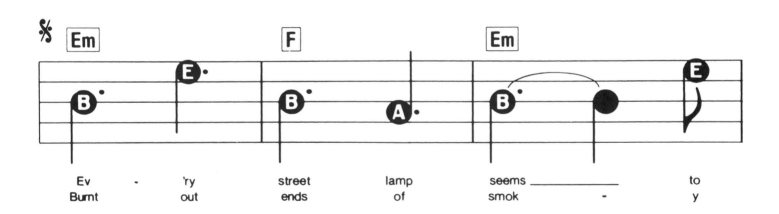

Ev - 'ry street lamp seems _____ to
Burnt out ends of smok - y

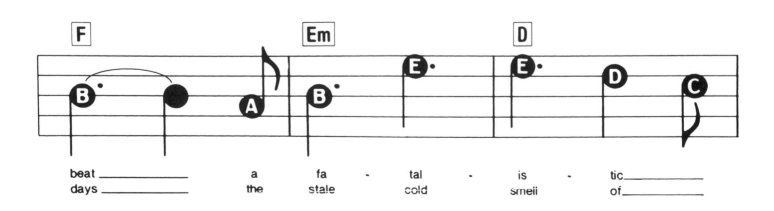

beat _____ a fa - tal - is - tic _____
days _____ the stale cold smell of _____

# Mona Lisa
## from the Paramount Picture CAPTAIN CAREY, U.S.A.

Registration 9
Rhythm: Swing

Words and Music by Jay Livingston
and Ray Evans

Mo - na Li - sa, Mo - na Li - sa, men have

named you. You're so like the la - dy with the mys - tic

smile. Is it on - ly 'cause you're lone - ly they have

blamed you for that Mo - na Li - sa strange - ness in your

smile? Do you smile to tempt a lov - er, Mo - na

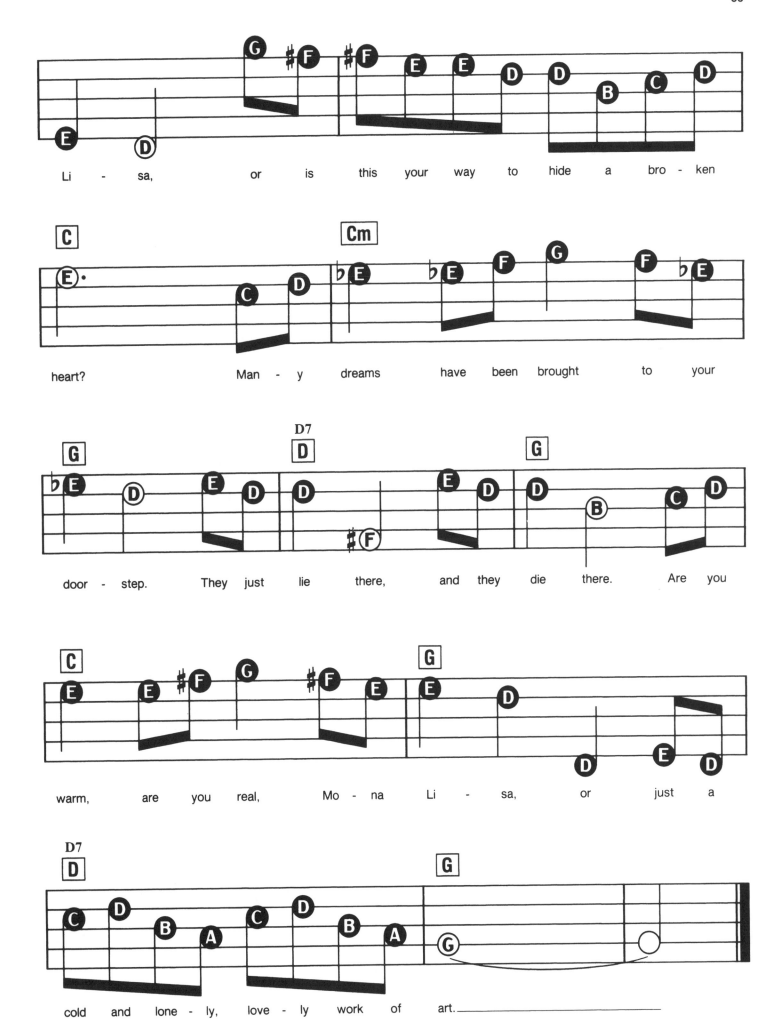

# Mood Indigo
## from SOPHISTICATED LADIES

Registration 4
Rhythm: Swing or Ballad

Words and Music by Duke Ellington,
Irving Mills and Albany Bigard

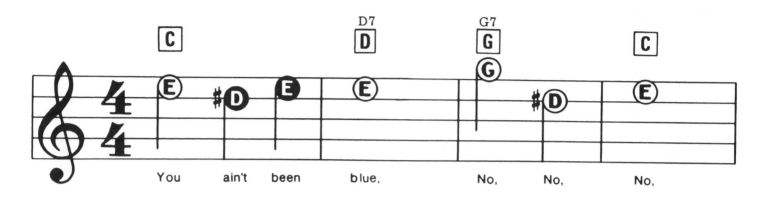

You ain't been blue, No, No, No,

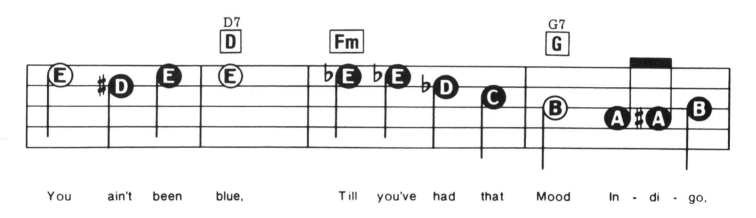

You ain't been blue, Till you've had that Mood In - di - go,

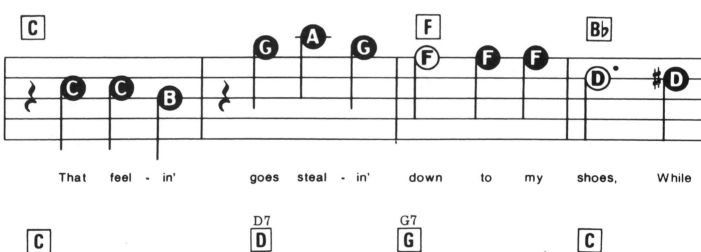

That feel - in' goes steal - in' down to my shoes, While

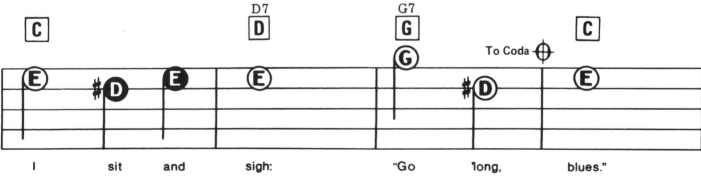

I sit and sigh: "Go 'long, blues."

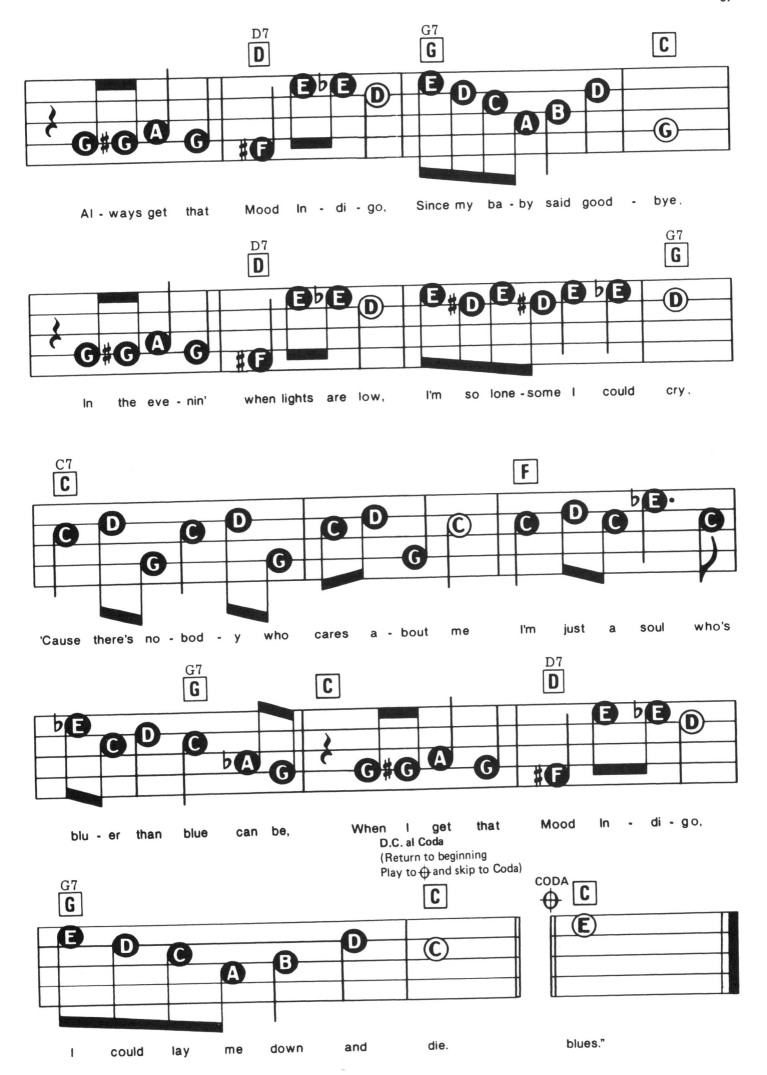

# Moon River
## from the Paramount Picture BREAKFAST AT TIFFANY'S

Registration 7
Rhythm: Waltz

Words by Johnny Mercer
Music by Henry Mancini

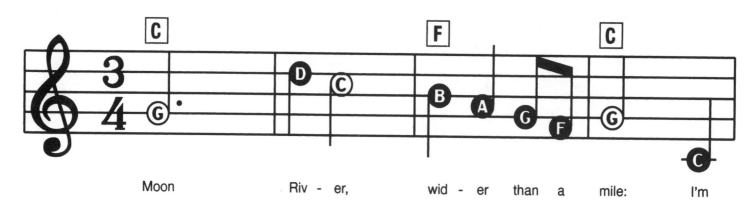

Moon River, wider than a mile: I'm

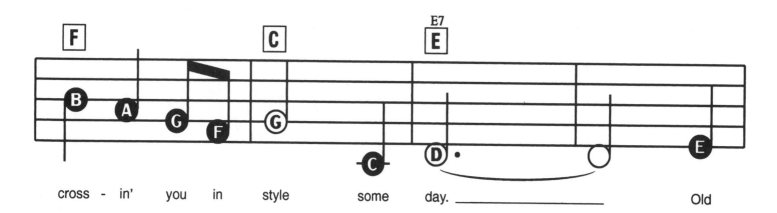

cross - in' you in style some day. _____ Old

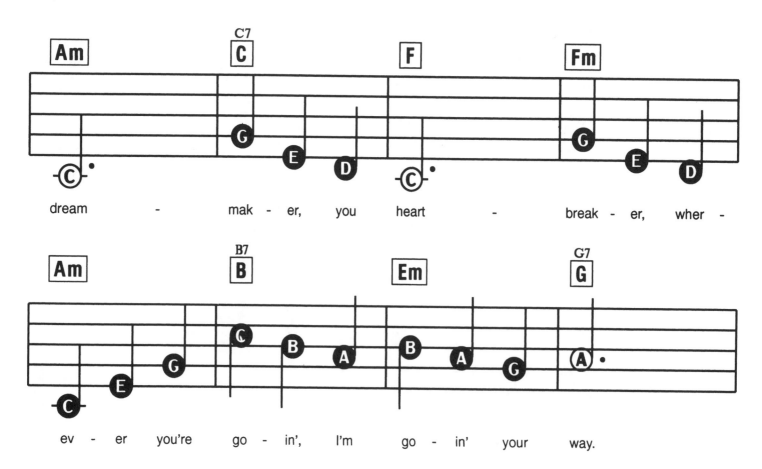

dream - mak - er, you heart - break - er, wher -

ev - er you're go - in', I'm go - in' your way.

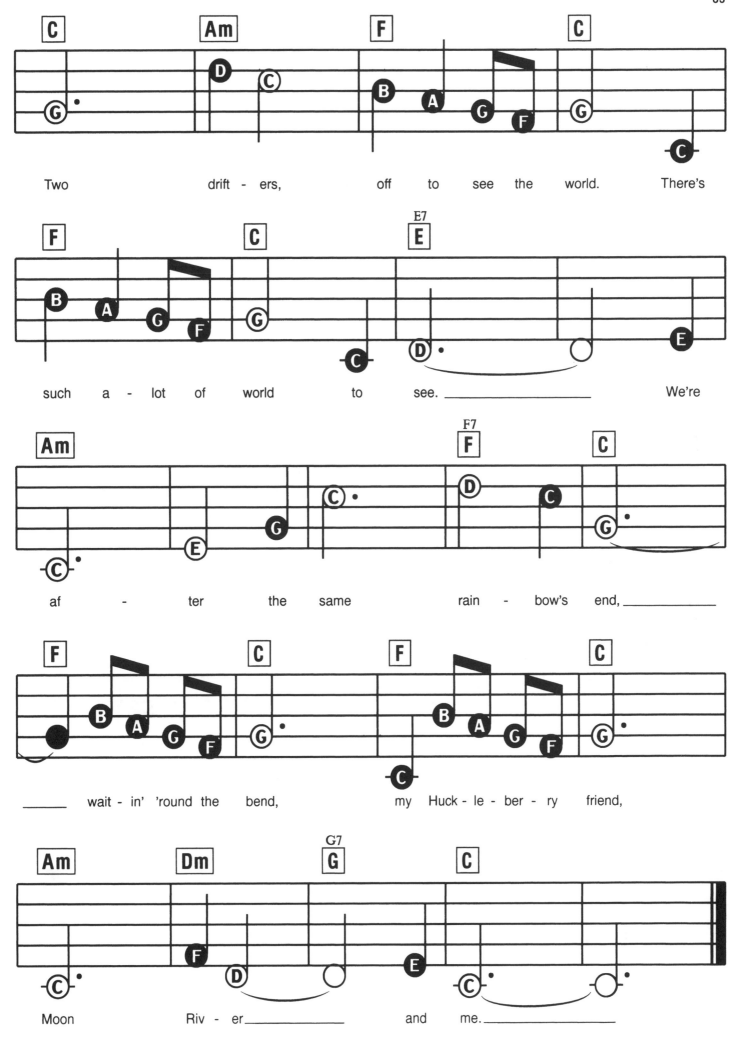

# Moonglow

Registration 2
Rhythm: Fox Trot

Words and Music by Will Hudson,
Eddie De Lange and Irving Mills

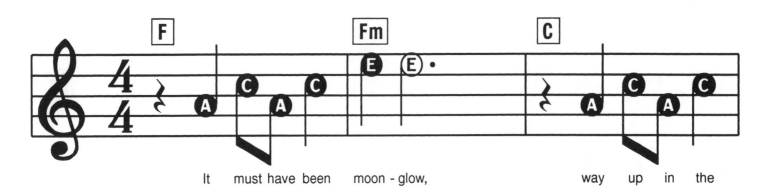

It must have been moon - glow,           way up in the

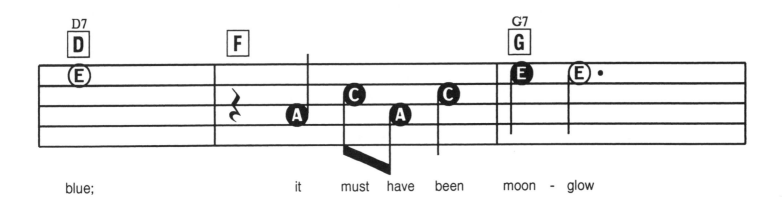

blue;           it must have been moon - glow

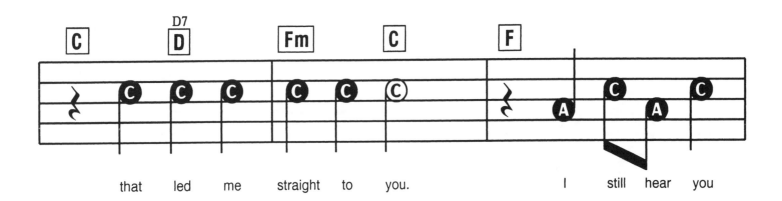

that led me straight to you.           I still hear you

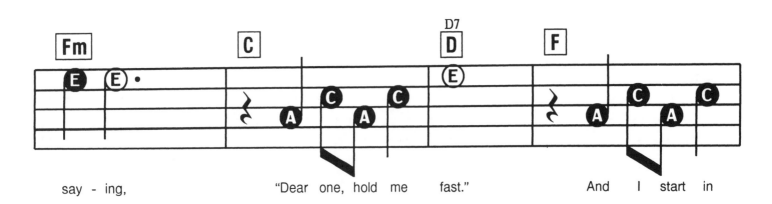

say - ing,           "Dear one, hold me fast."           And I start in

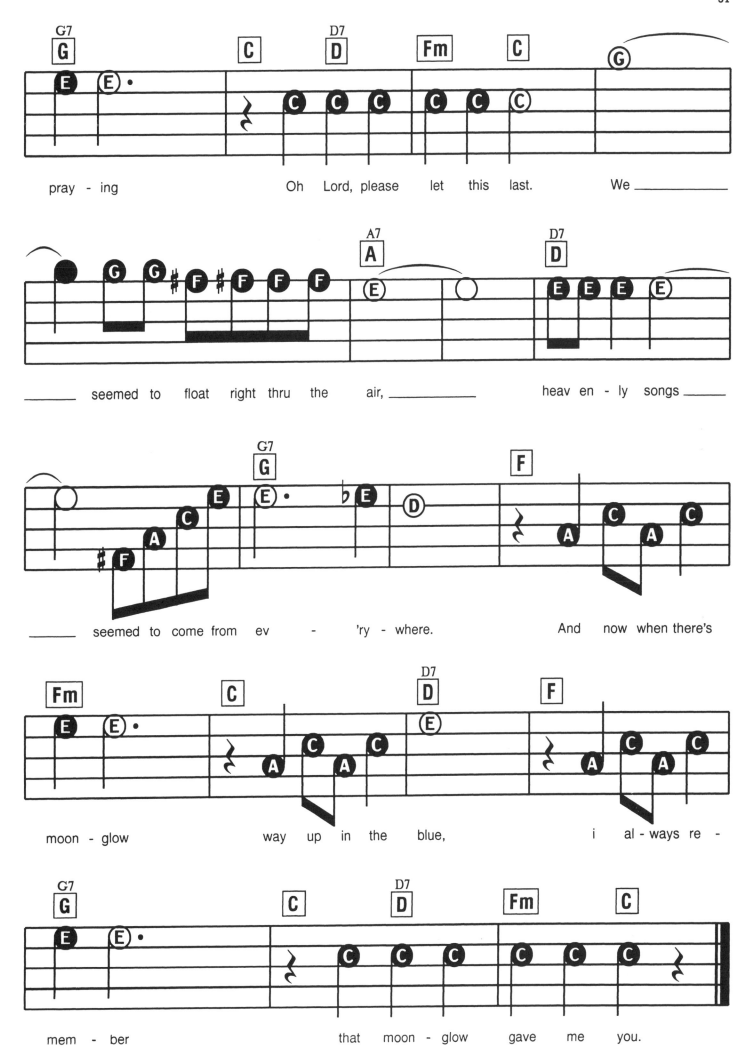

# Moonlight in Vermont

Registration 2
Rhythm: Fox Trot or Swing

Words and Music by John Blackburn
and Karl Suessdorf

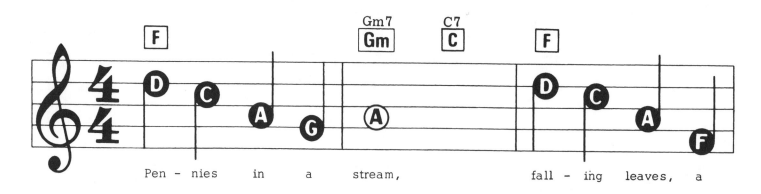

Pen - nies in a stream, fall - ing leaves, a

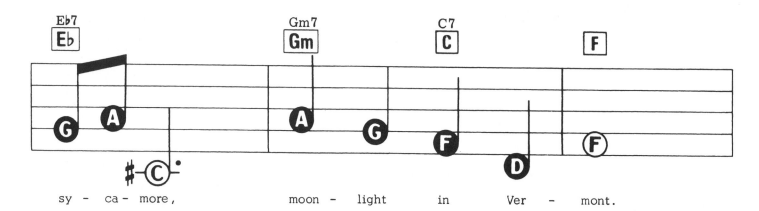

sy - ca - more, moon - light in Ver - mont.

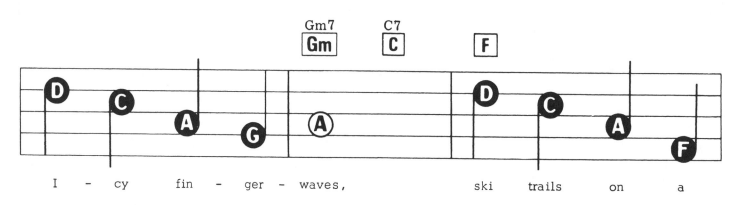

I - cy fin - ger - waves, ski trails on a

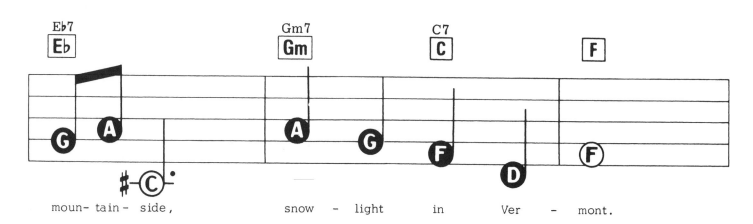

moun - tain - side, snow - light in Ver - mont.

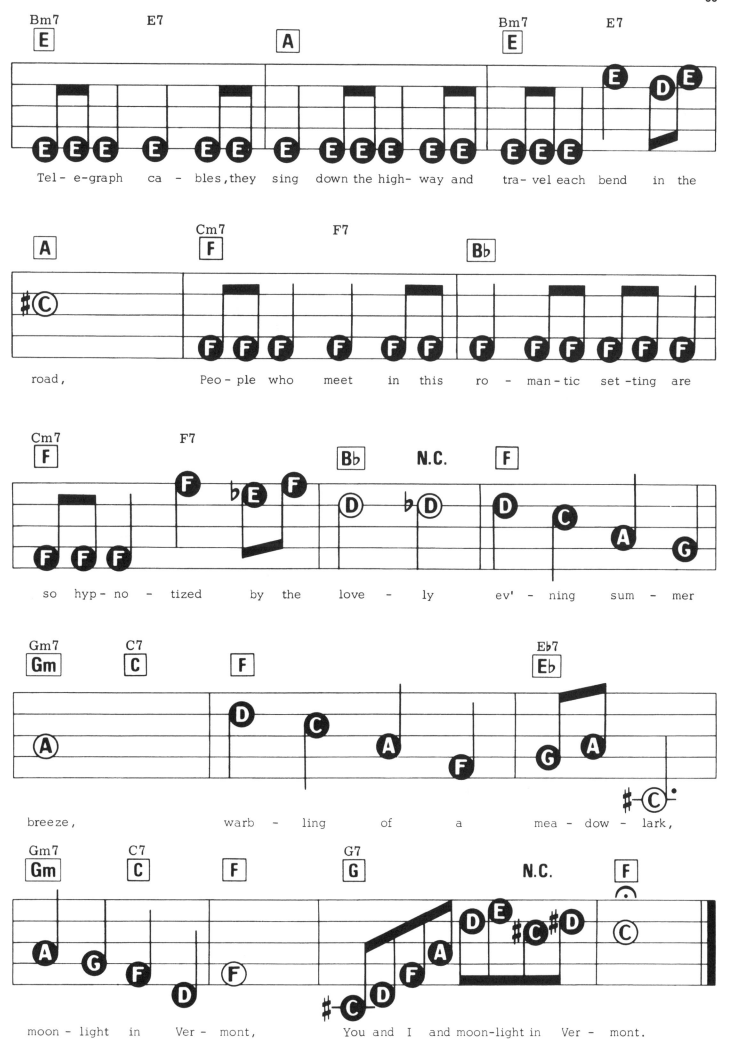

# More
## (Ti Guarderò Nel Cuore)
## from the Film MONDO CANE

Registration 2
Rhythm: Bossa Nova or Latin

Music by Nino Oliviero and Riz Ortolani
Italian Lyrics by Marcello Ciorciolini
English Lyrics by Norman Newell

More than the great-est love the world has known,

This is the love I'll give to you a - lone;

More than the sim - ple words I try to say,

I on - ly live to love you more each

day. More than you'll ev - er know, my

95

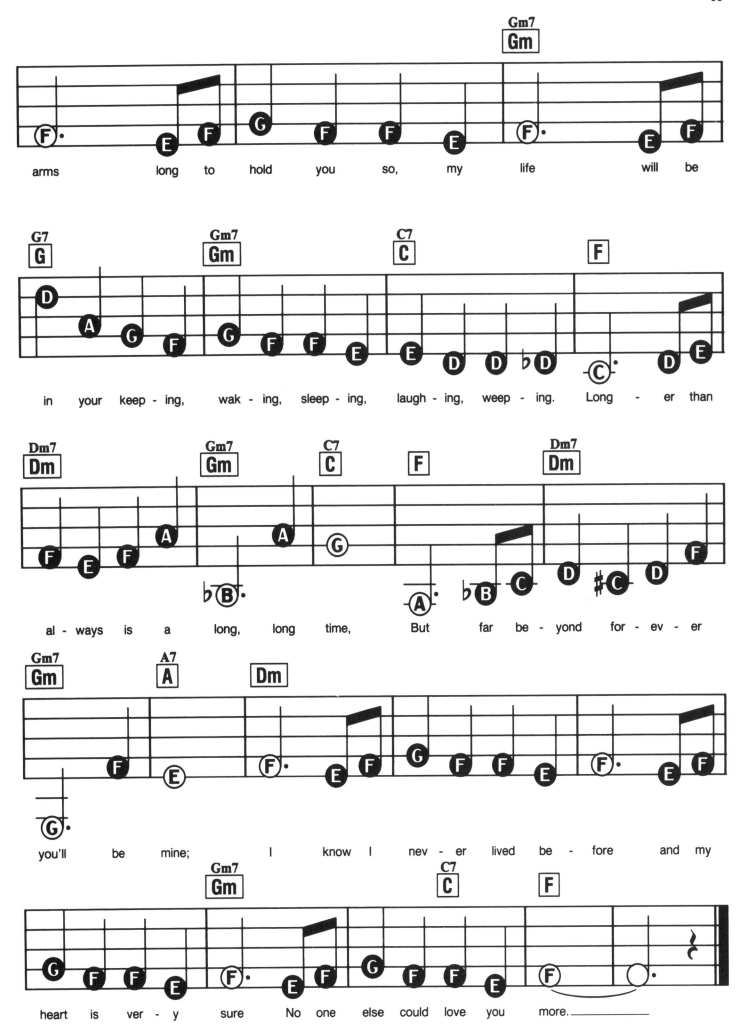

# My Favorite Things
## from THE SOUND OF MUSIC

Registration 9
Rhythm: Waltz

Lyrics by Oscar Hammerstein II
Music by Richard Rodgers

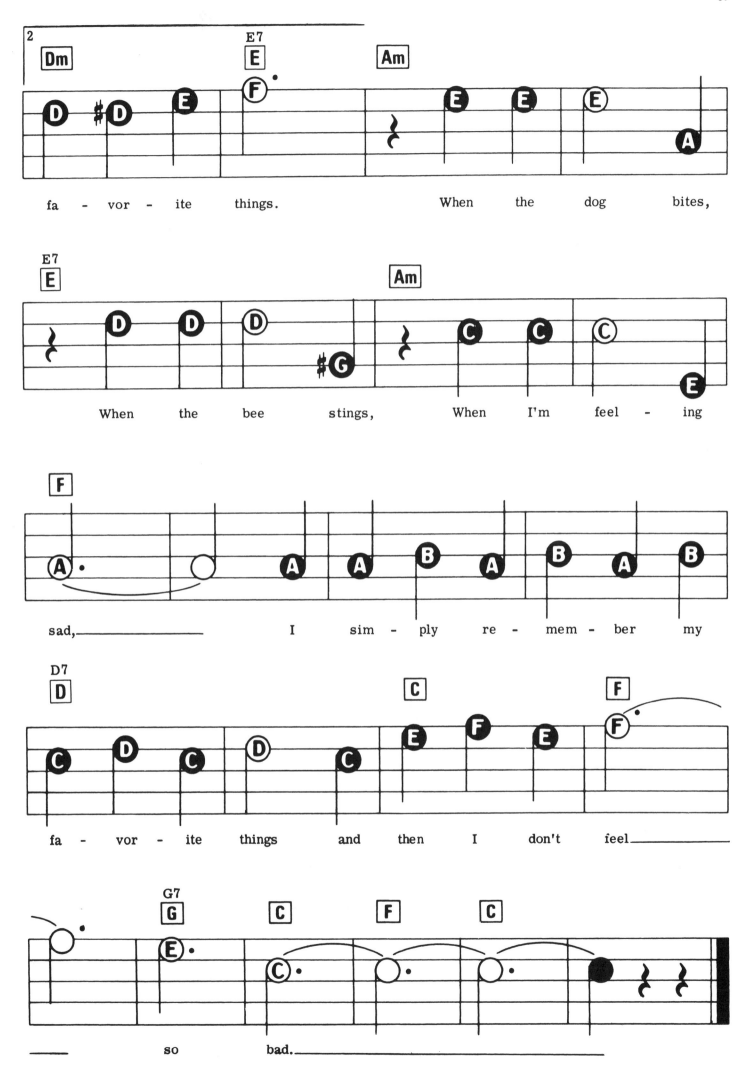

# My Funny Valentine
## from BABES IN ARMS

Registration 1
Rhythm: Ballad

Words by Lorenz Hart
Music by Richard Rodgers

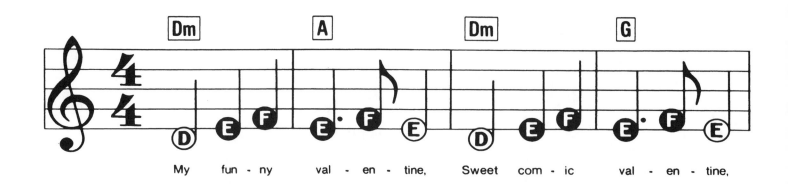

My fun - ny val - en - tine, Sweet com - ic val - en - tine,

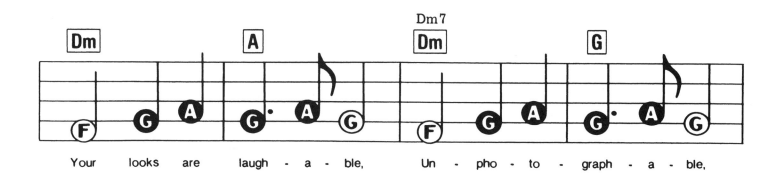

You make me smile with my heart. _____

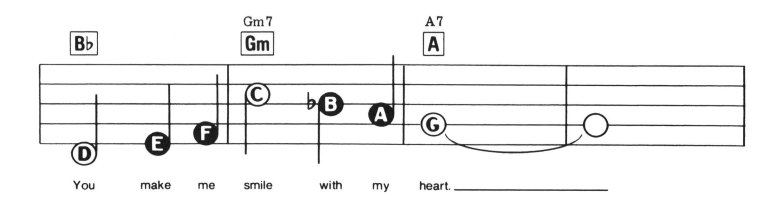

Your looks are laugh - a - ble, Un - pho - to - graph - a - ble,

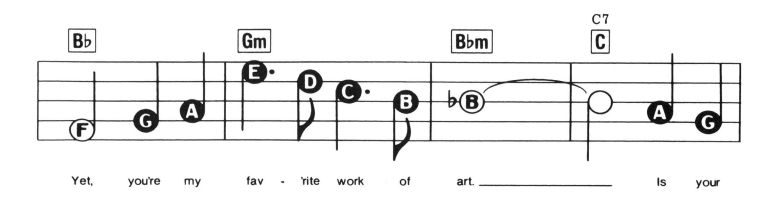

Yet, you're my fav - 'rite work of art. _____ Is your

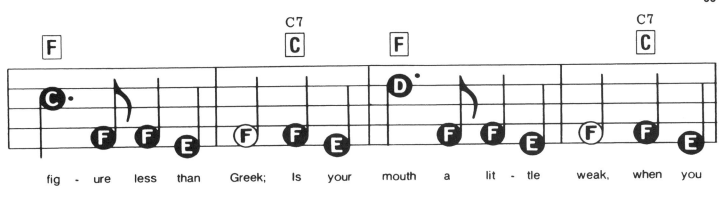

fig - ure less than Greek; Is your mouth a lit - tle weak, when you

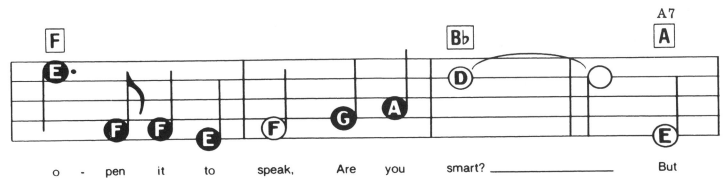

o - pen it to speak, Are you smart? _____ But

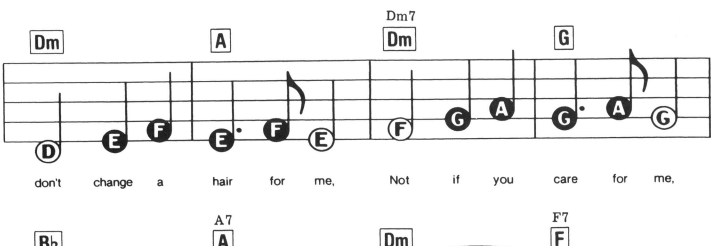

don't change a hair for me, Not if you care for me,

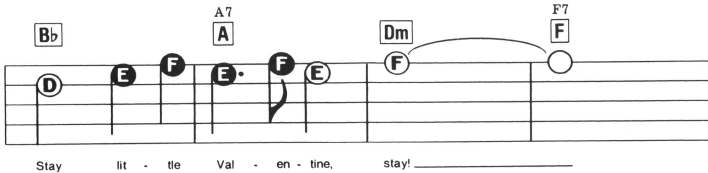

Stay lit - tle Val - en - tine, stay! _____

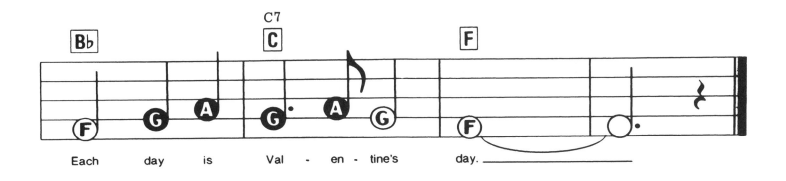

Each day is Val - en - tine's day. _____

# Ol' Man River
### from SHOW BOAT

Registration 5
Rhythm: Ballad or Fox Trot

Lyrics by Oscar Hammerstein II
Music by Jerome Kern

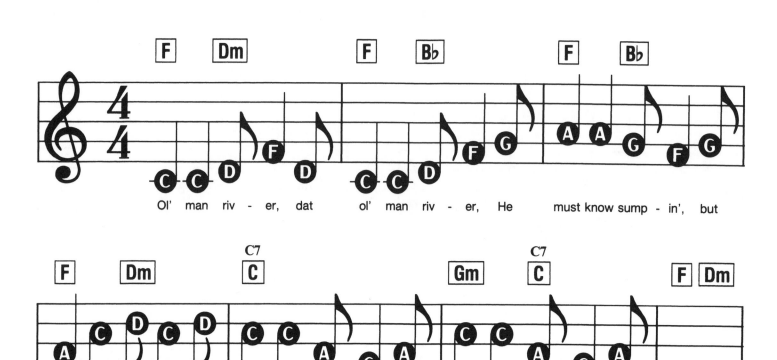

Ol' man riv - er, dat ol' man riv - er, He must know sump - in', but

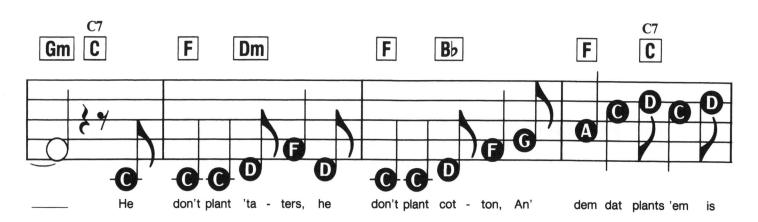

don't say noth - in', He jus' keeps roll - in', He keeps on roll - in' a - long.

He don't plant 'ta - ters, he don't plant cot - ton, An' dem dat plants 'em is

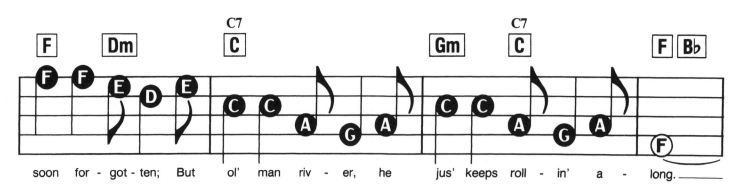

soon for - got - ten; But ol' man riv - er, he jus' keeps roll - in' a - long.

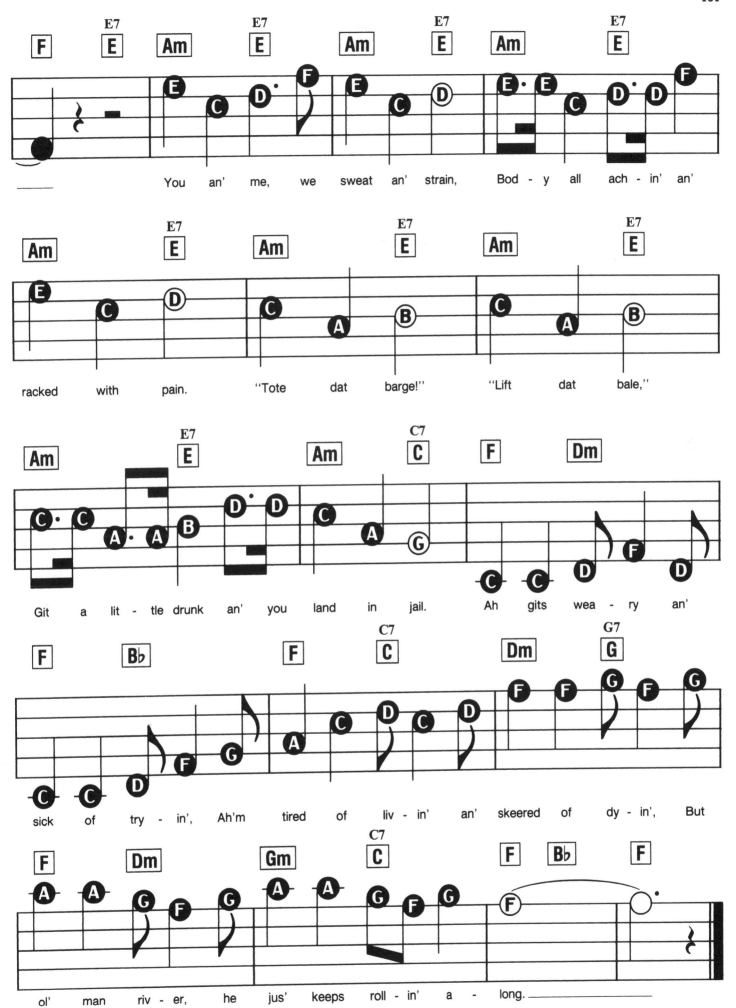

# On the Street Where You Live
### from MY FAIR LADY

Registration 4
Rhythm: Beguine

Words by Alan Jay Lerner
Music by Frederick Loewe

I have of-ten walked down this street be-fore But the
li - lac trees in the heart of town? Can you
stop and stare, they don't both-er me; For there's

pave-ment al - ways stayed be-neath my feet be-fore. All at
hear a lark in an - y oth - er part of town? Does en -
no-where else on earth that I would rath - er be. Let the

once am I sev - 'ral stor - ies high, Know - ing
chant - ment pour out of ev - 'ry door? No, it's
time go by, I won't care if I can be

I'm on the street where you live. Are there
just on the
here on the

street where you live. And

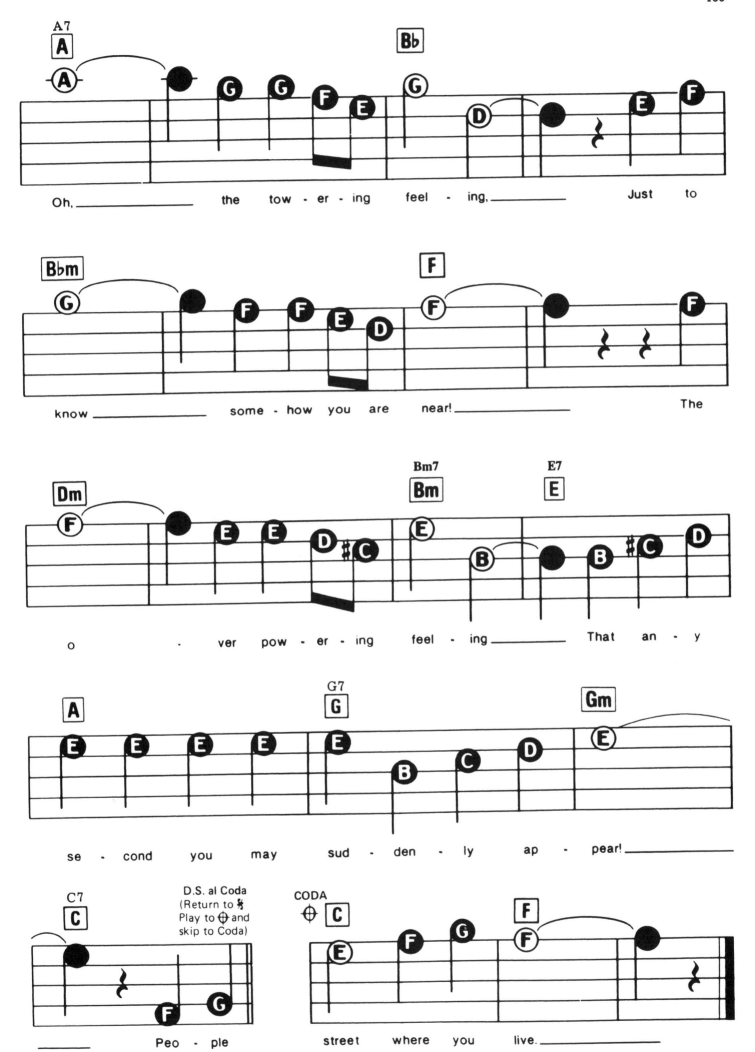

# People
## from FUNNY GIRL

Registration 1
Rhythm: Ballad or Fox Trot

Words by Bob Merrill
Music by Jule Styne

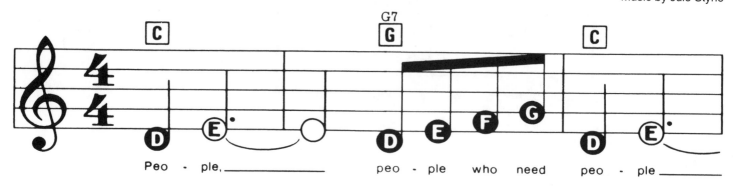

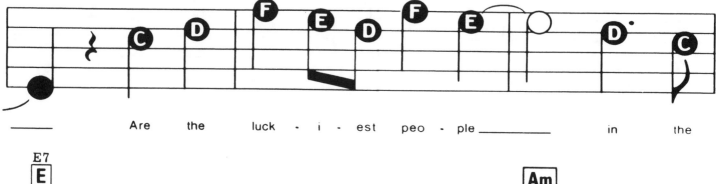

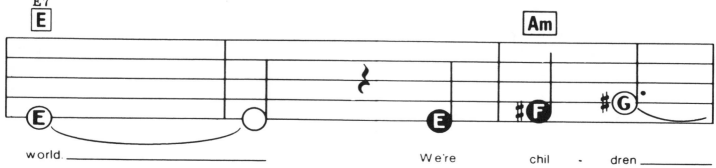

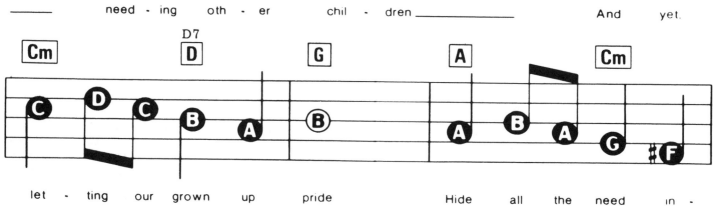

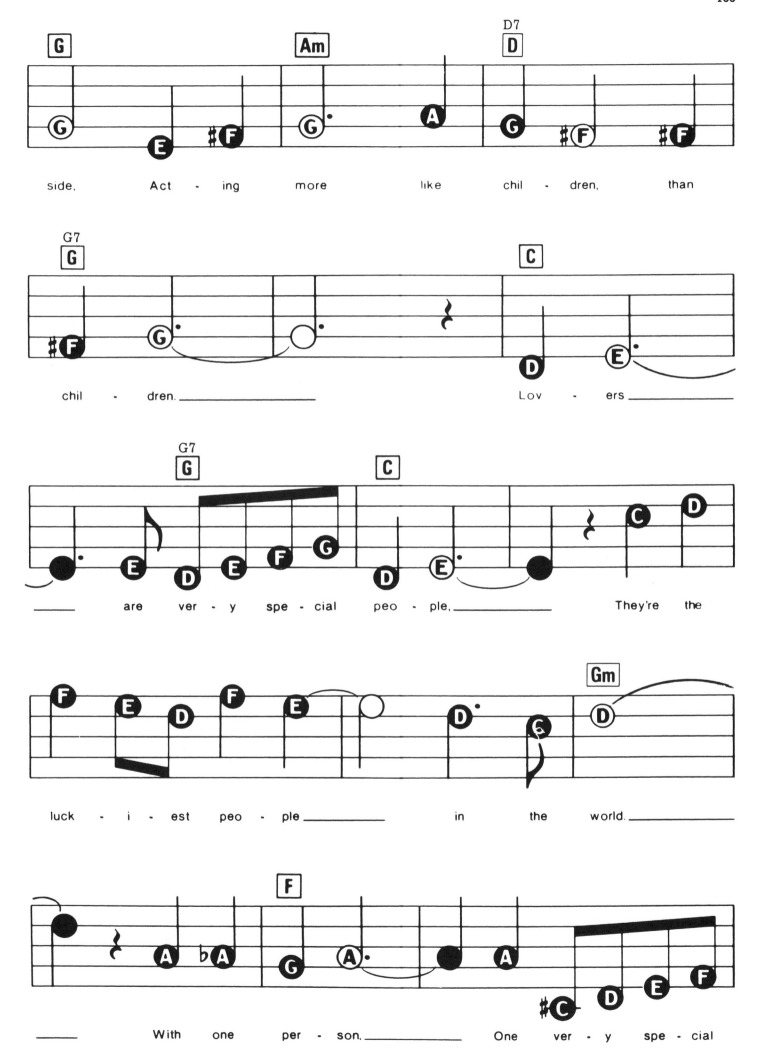

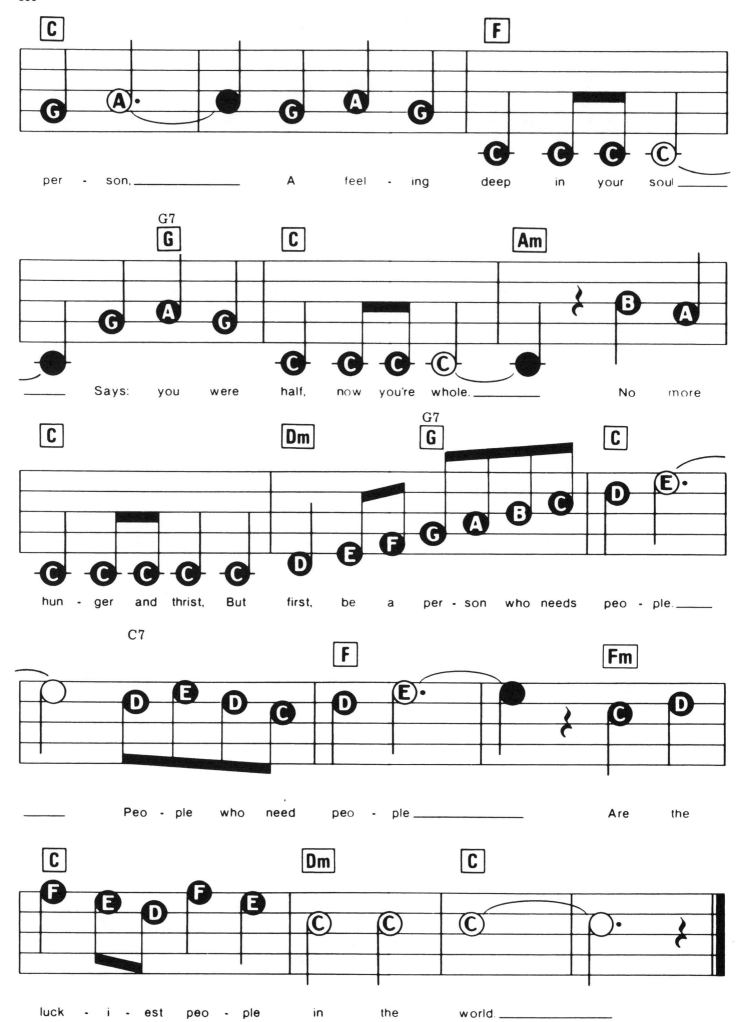

# Piano Man

Registration 4
Rhythm: Waltz

Words and Music by
Billy Joel

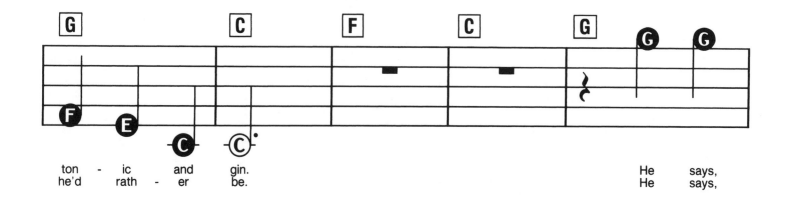

ton - ic and gin.
he'd rath - er be.
He says,
He says,

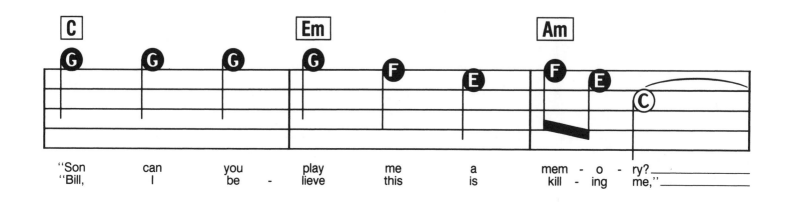

"Son can you play me a mem - o - ry?
"Bill, I be - lieve me this is kill - ing me,"

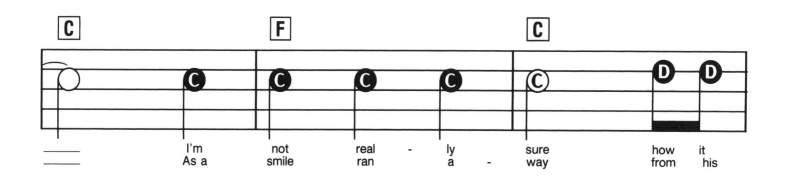

I'm not real - ly sure how it
As a smile ran a - way from his

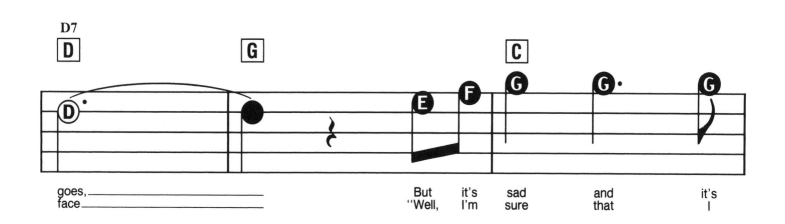

goes,
face
But it's sad and it's
"Well, I'm sure that I

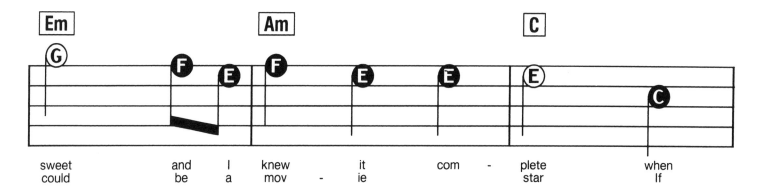

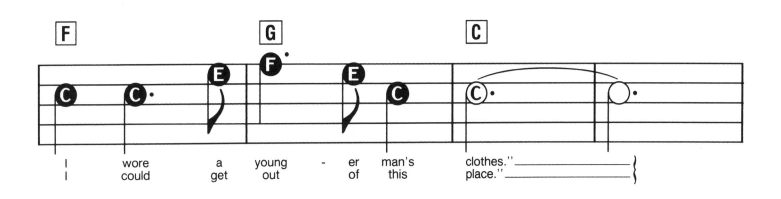

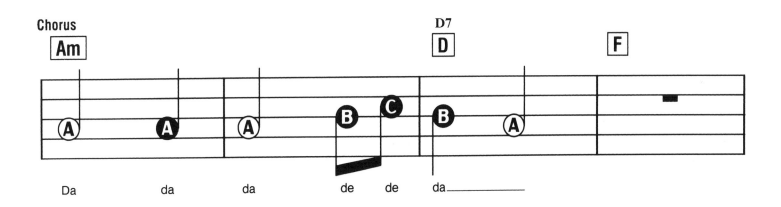

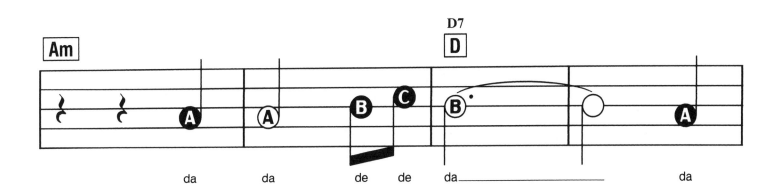

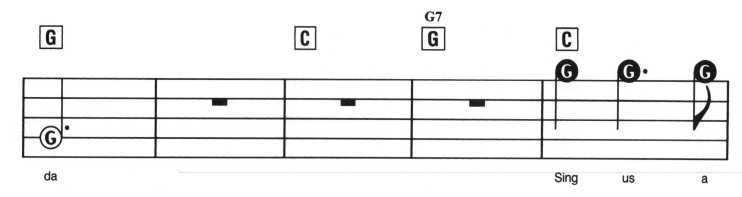

da ................................................ Sing us a

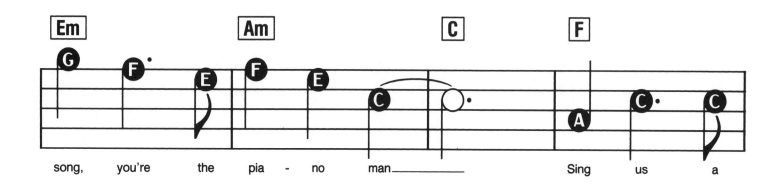

song, you're the pia - no man _____ Sing us a

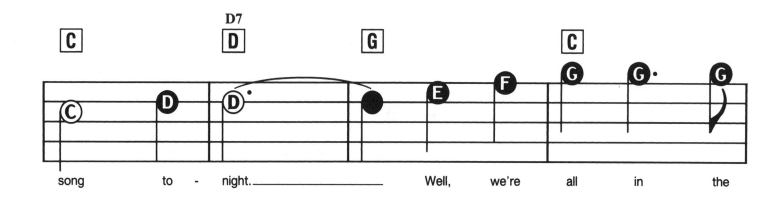

song to - night. _____ Well, we're all in the

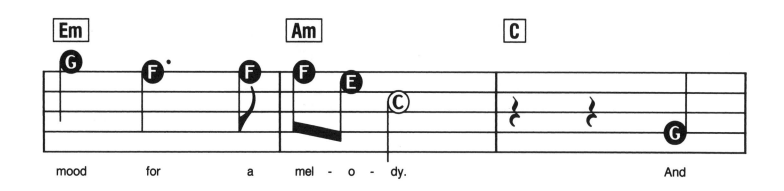

mood for a mel - o - dy. And

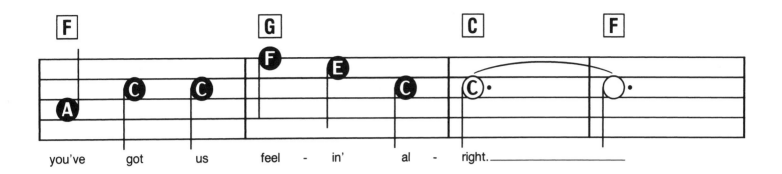

you've got us feel - in' al - right.____

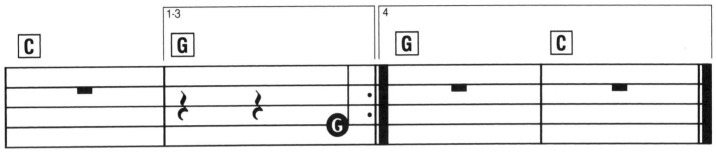

2. Now
3. Now
4. It's a

## Additional Lyrics

**3.** Now Paul is a real estate novelist,
Who never had time for a wife,
And he's talkin' with Davey who's still in the Navy
And probably will be for life.
And the waitress is practicing politics,
As the businessmen slowly get stoned
Yes, they're sharing a drink they call loneliness
But it's better than drinkin' alone.

*CHORUS*

**4.** It's a pretty good crowd for a Saturday,
And the manager gives me a smile
'Cause he knows that it's me they've been comin' to see
To forget about life for a while.
And the piano sounds like a carnival
And the microphone smells like a beer
And they sit at the bar and put bread in my jar
And say "Man, what are you doin' here?"

*CHORUS*

# The Rainbow Connection
## from THE MUPPET MOVIE

Registration 4
Rhythm: Waltz

Words and Music by Paul Williams
and Kenneth L. Ascher

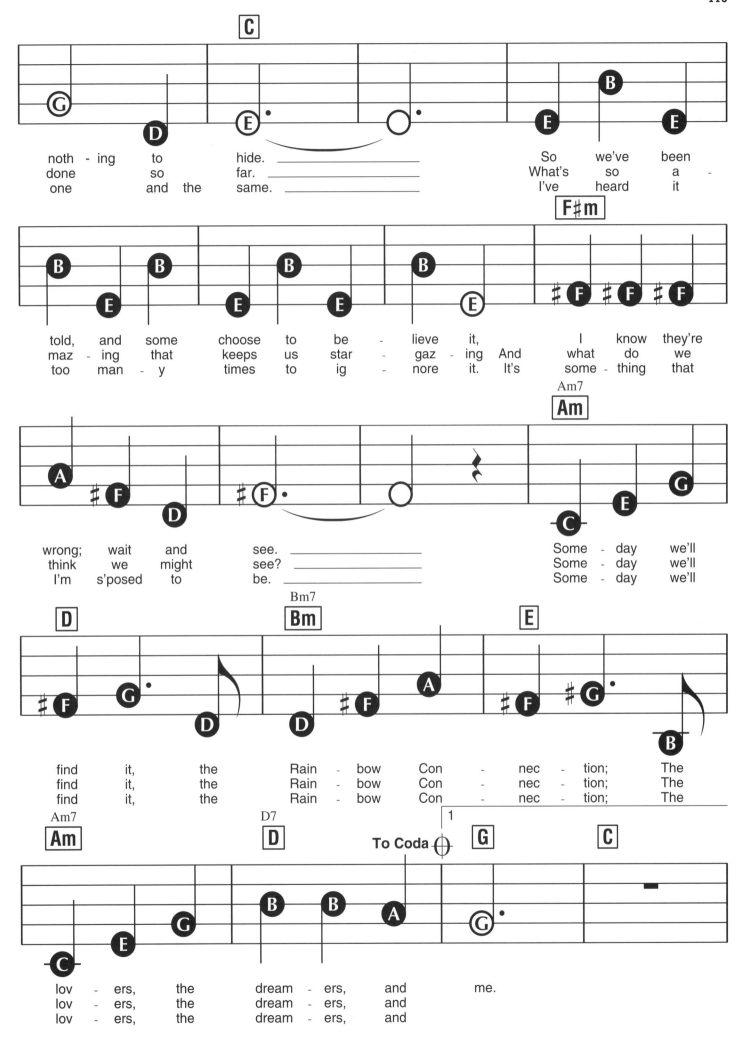

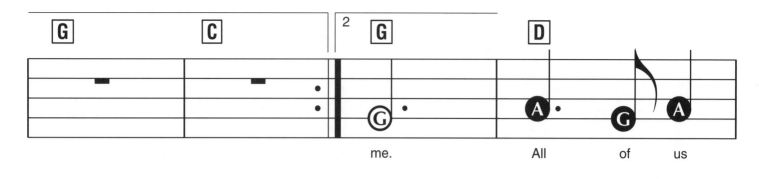

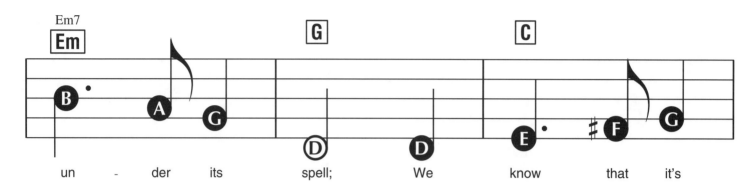

me.      All    of    us

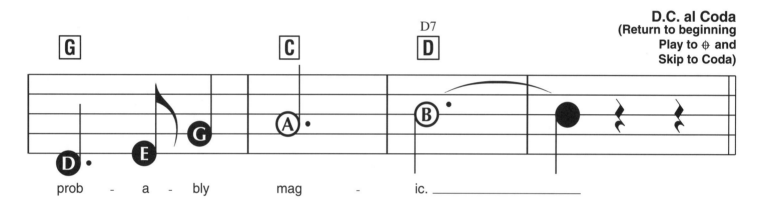

un - der its    spell;    We    know    that    it's

**D.C. al Coda**
**(Return to beginning**
**Play to ⊕ and**
**Skip to Coda)**

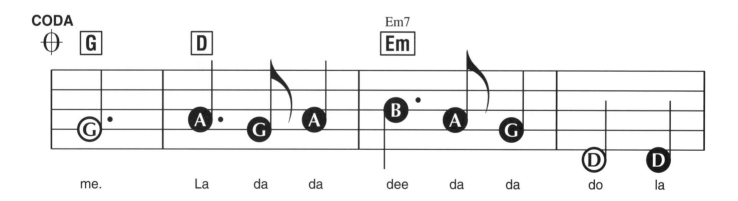

prob - a - bly    mag - ic. _____

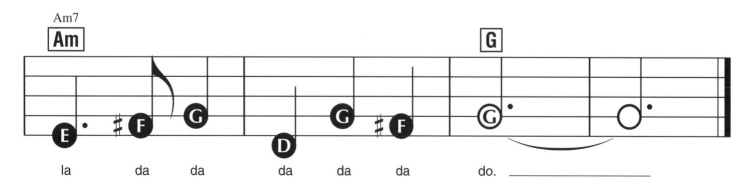

me.    La    da    da    dee    da    da    do    la

la    da    da    da    da    da    do. _____

# Spanish Eyes

Registration 3
Rhythm: Latin or Bossa Nova

Words by Charles Singleton and Eddie Snyder
Music by Bert Kaempfert

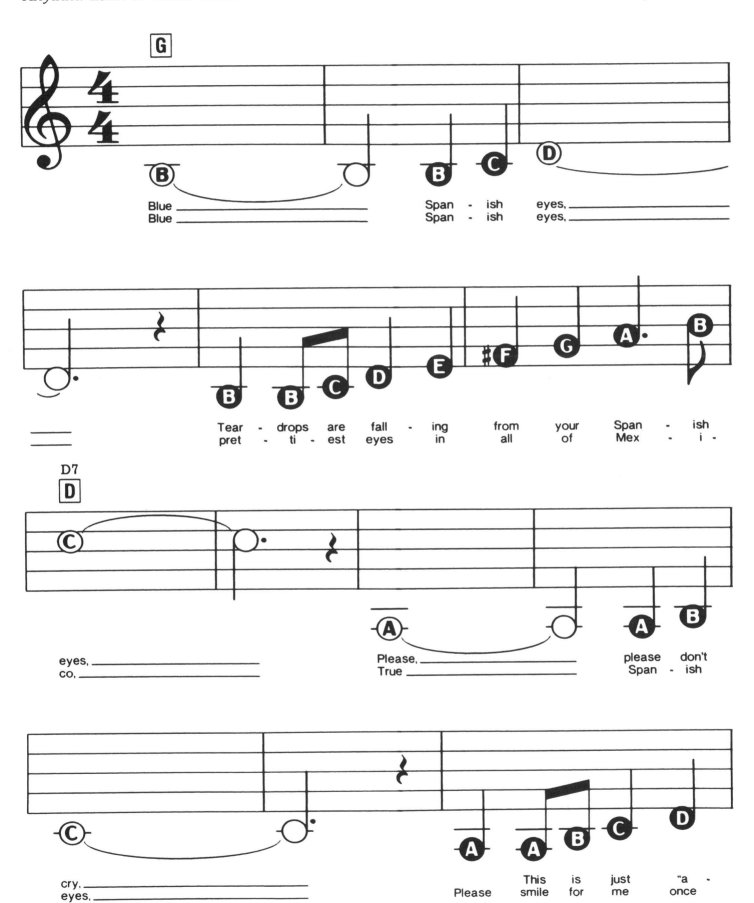

Blue _____ Span - ish eyes, _____
Blue _____ Span - ish eyes, _____

_____ Tear - drops are fall - ing from your Span - ish
_____ pret - ti - est eyes in all of Span Mex - i -

eyes, _____ Please, _____ please don't
co, _____ True _____ Span - ish

cry, _____ 
eyes, _____ Please This is just "a -
Please smile for me once

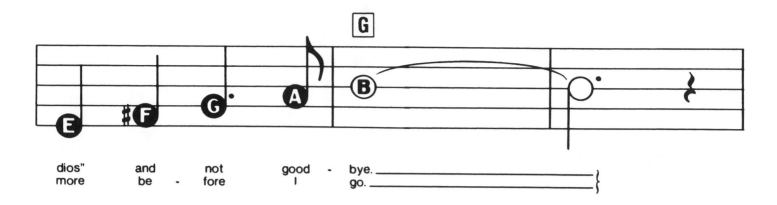

dios"  and  not  good - bye. _____
more  be - fore  I  go. _____

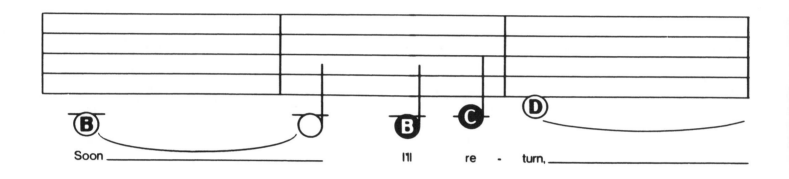

Soon _____  I'll  re - turn, _____

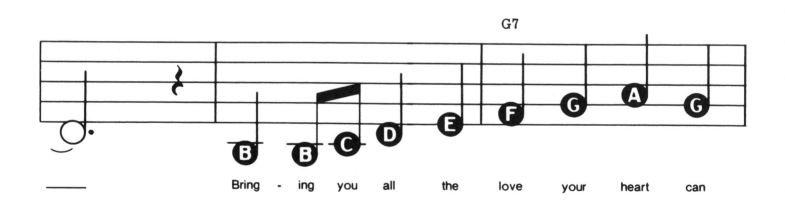

_____  Bring - ing  you  all  the  love  your  heart  can

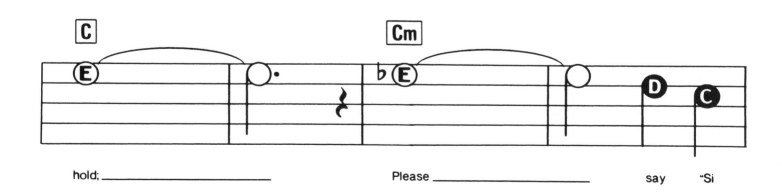

hold; _____  Please _____  say  "Si

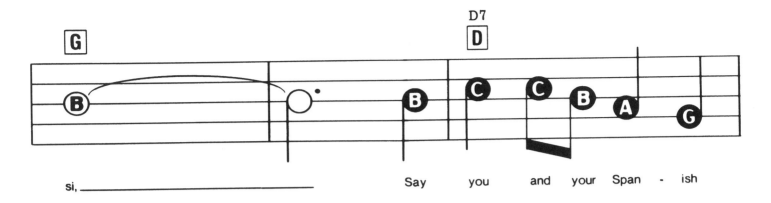

si, _____ Say you and your Span - ish

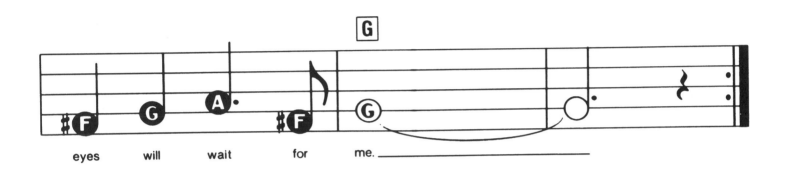

eyes will wait for me. _____

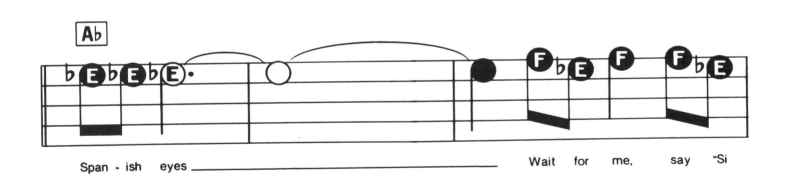

Span - ish eyes _____ Wait for me, say "Si

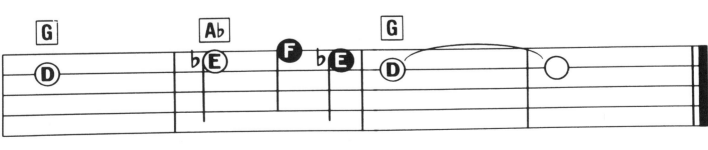

Si!" _____

# Satin Doll
## from SOPHISTICATED LADIES

Registration 4
Rhythm: Swing or Jazz

Words by Johnny Mercer and Billy Strayhorn
Music by Duke Ellington

Cig - a - rette hold - er, which wigs me,
Ba - by shall we go out skip - pin'

o - ver her shoul - der she digs me, out cat - tin'
care - ful a - mi - go, you're flip - pin', speaks Lat - in,

that sat - in doll.
that sat - in doll.

doll.

She's no - bod - y's fool, so I'm

# September Song
## from the Musical Play KNICKERBOCKER HOLIDAY

Registration 2
Rhythm: Fox Trot

Words by Maxwell Anderson
Music by Kurt Weill

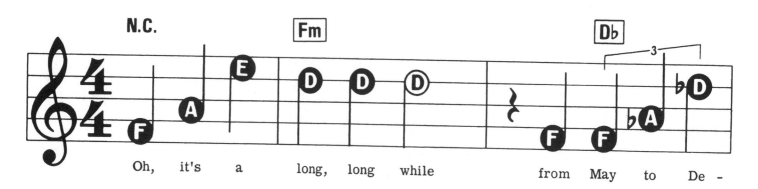

Oh, it's a long, long while from May to De-

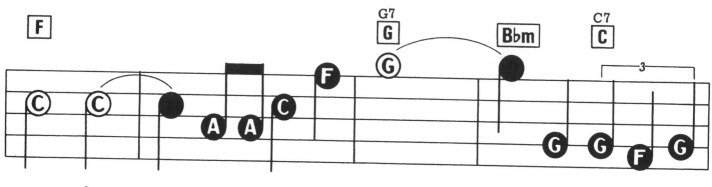

cem - ber,_____ But the days grow short,_____ when you reach Sep -

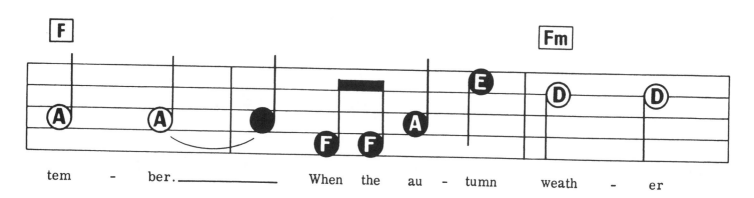

tem - ber._____ When the au - tumn weath - er

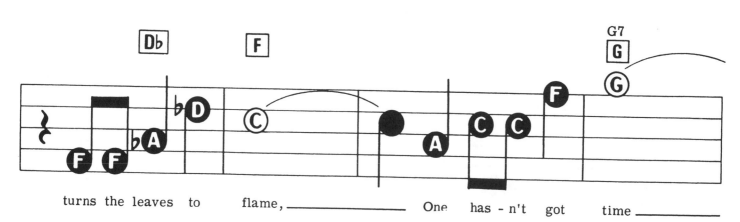

turns the leaves to flame,_____ One has - n't got time _____

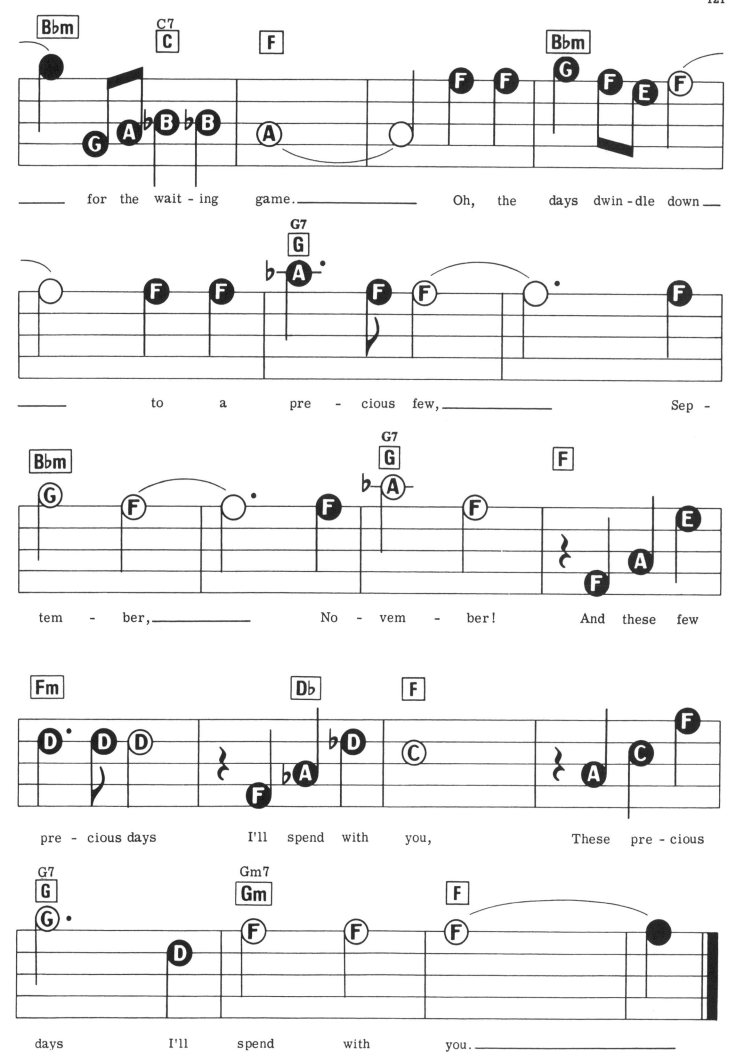

# Some Day My Prince Will Come

Registration 2
Rhythm: Waltz

Words by Larry Morey
Music by Frank Churchill

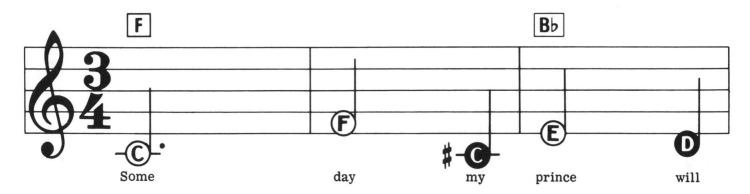

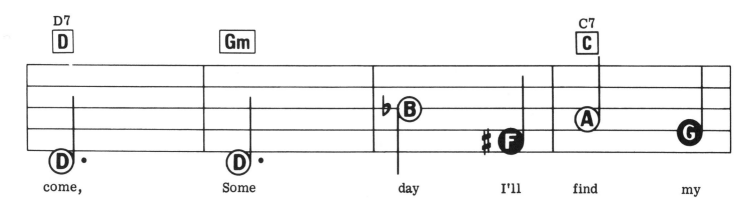

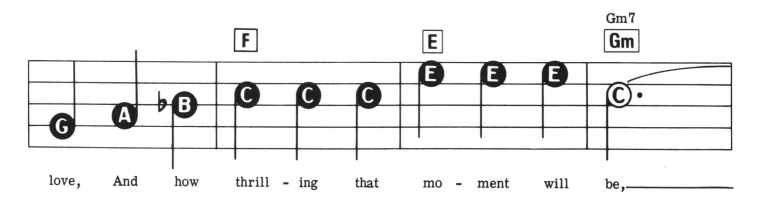

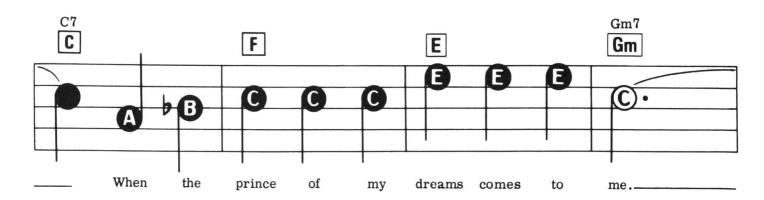

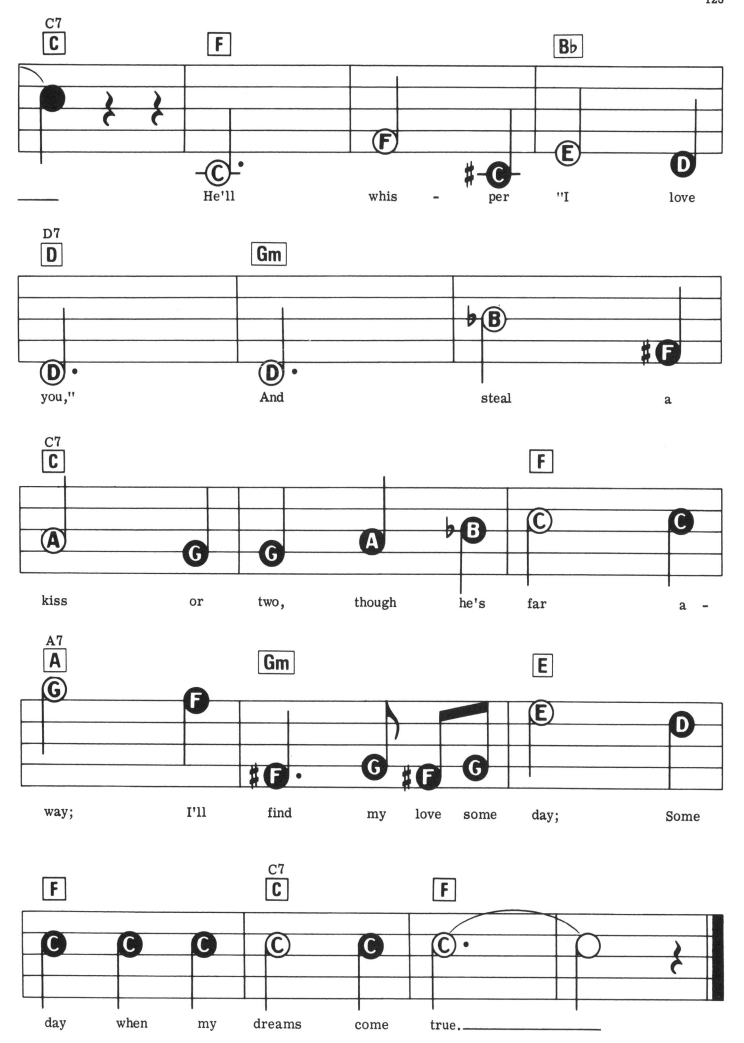

# The Sound of Music
## from THE SOUND OF MUSIC

Registration 5
Rhythm: Fox Trot

Lyrics by Oscar Hammerstein II
Music by Richard Rodgers

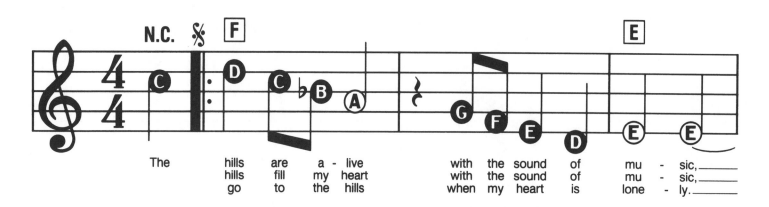

The hills are a-live with the sound of mu - sic,
hills fill my heart with the sound of mu - sic,
go to the hills when my heart is lone - ly.

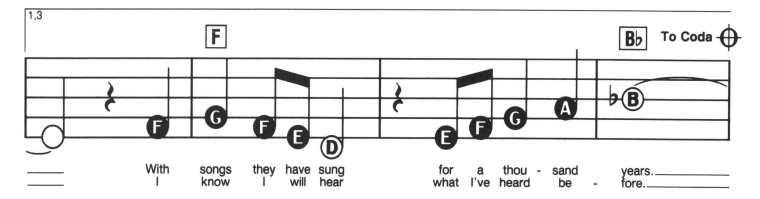

With songs they have sung for a thou - sand years.
I know I will hear what I've heard be - fore.

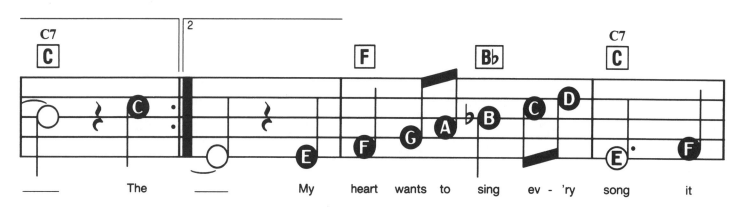

The My heart wants to sing ev - 'ry song it

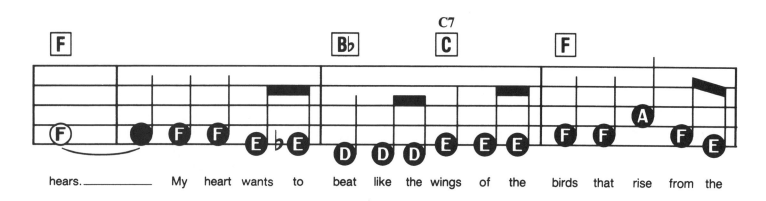

hears. My heart wants to beat like the wings of the birds that rise from the

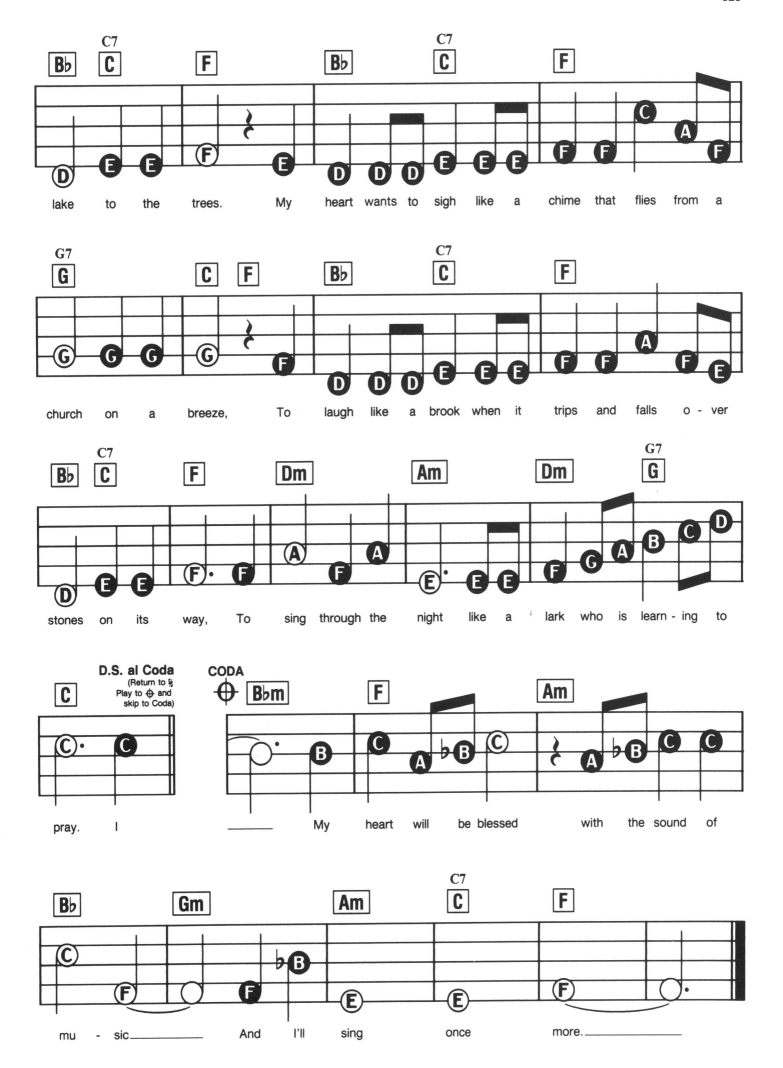

# Speak Softly, Love
## (Love Theme)
### from the Paramount Picture THE GODFATHER

Registration 1
Rhythm: Ballad or Slow Rock

Words by Larry Kusik
Music by Nino Rota

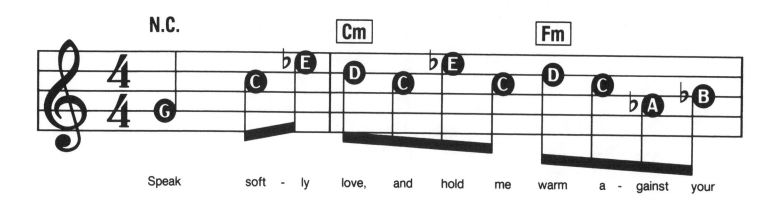

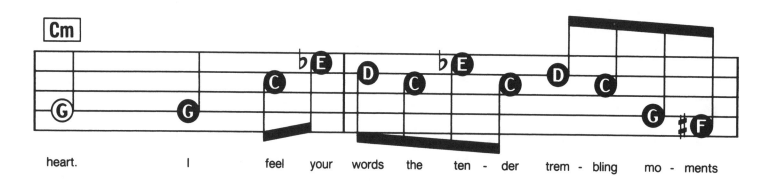

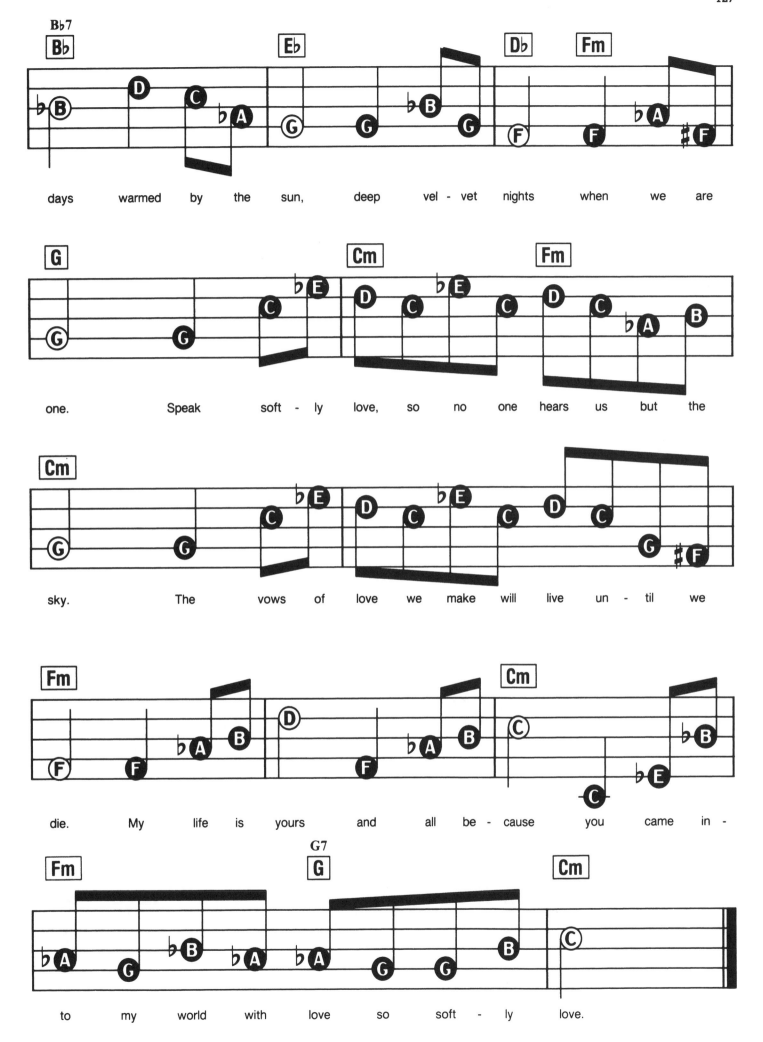

# Stardust

Registration 5
Rhythm: Swing or Jazz

Words by Mitchell Parish
Music by Hoagy Carmichael

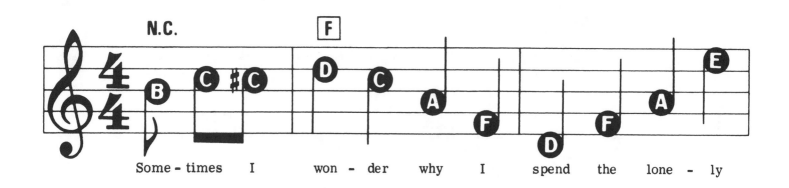

Some - times I won - der why I spend the lone - ly

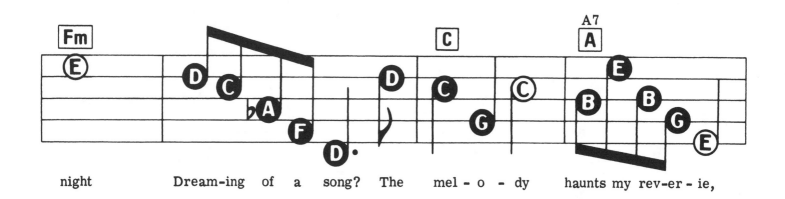

night  Dream-ing of a song? The mel - o - dy haunts my rev-er - ie,

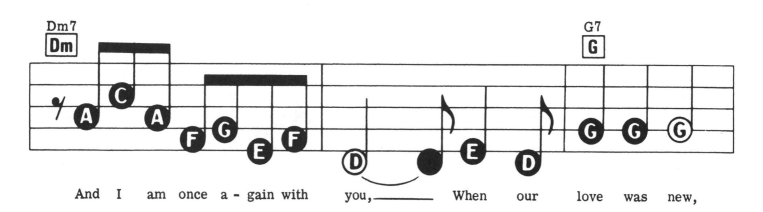

And I am once a - gain with  you,_____ When our love was new,

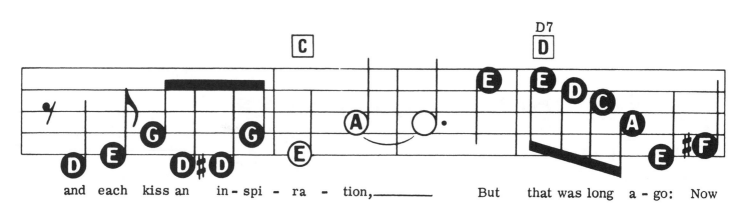

and each kiss an in - spi - ra - tion,_____ But that was long a - go: Now

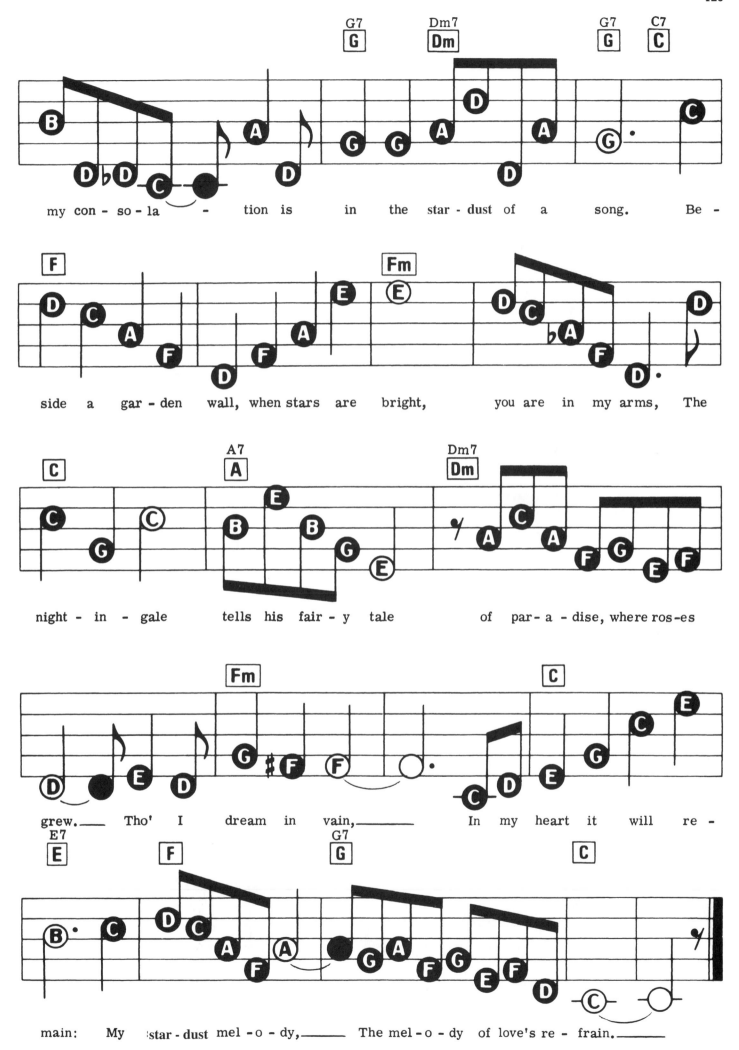

# Stormy Weather
## (Keeps Rainin' All the Time)
### from COTTON CLUB PARADE OF 1933

Registration 2
Rhythm: Ballad or R&B

Lyric by Ted Koehler
Music by Harold Arlen

Don't know why there's no sun up in the sky, storm-y
bare, gloom and mis-'ry ev-'ry-where, storm-y

weath-er, Since my man and I ain't to-geth-er,
weath-er, Just can't get my poor self to-geth-er,

keeps rain-in' all the time. _____
I'm wear-y all the

Life is

time, _____ the time, _____ So wear-y all the time. _____

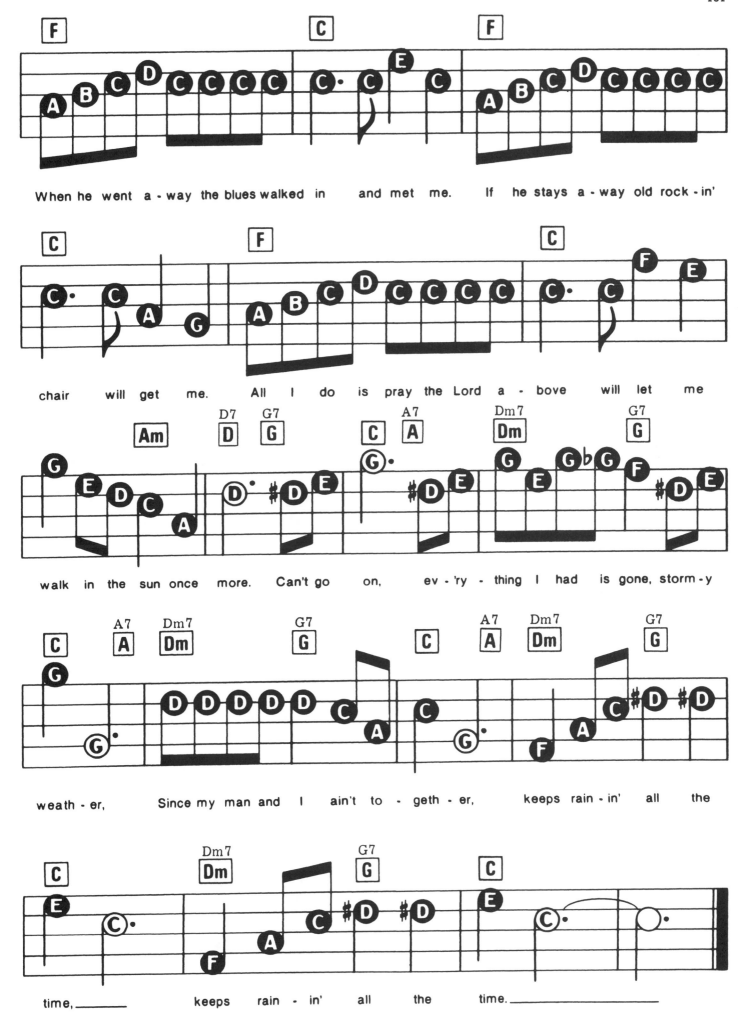

# A String of Pearls
## from THE GLENN MILLER STORY

Registration 4
Rhythm: Swing

Words by Eddie De Lange
Music by Jerry Gray

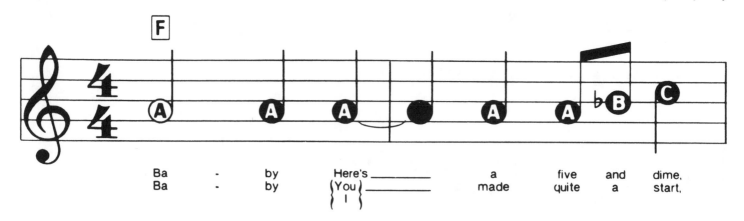

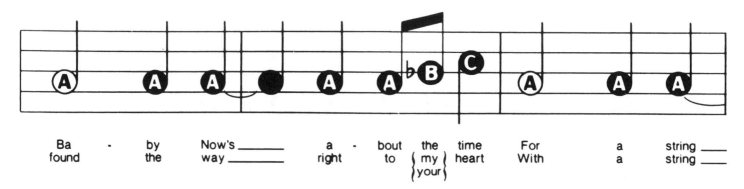

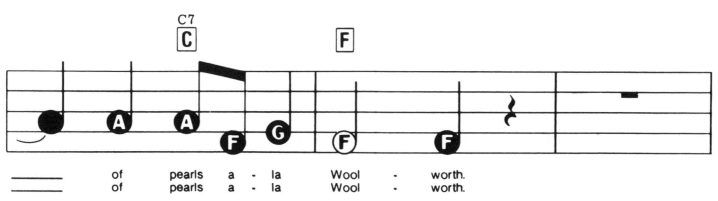

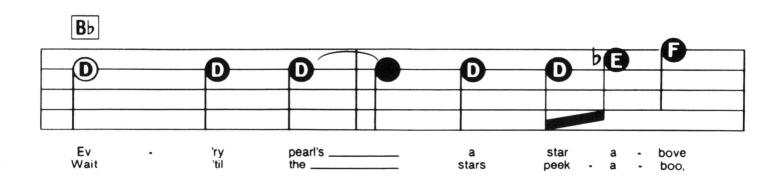

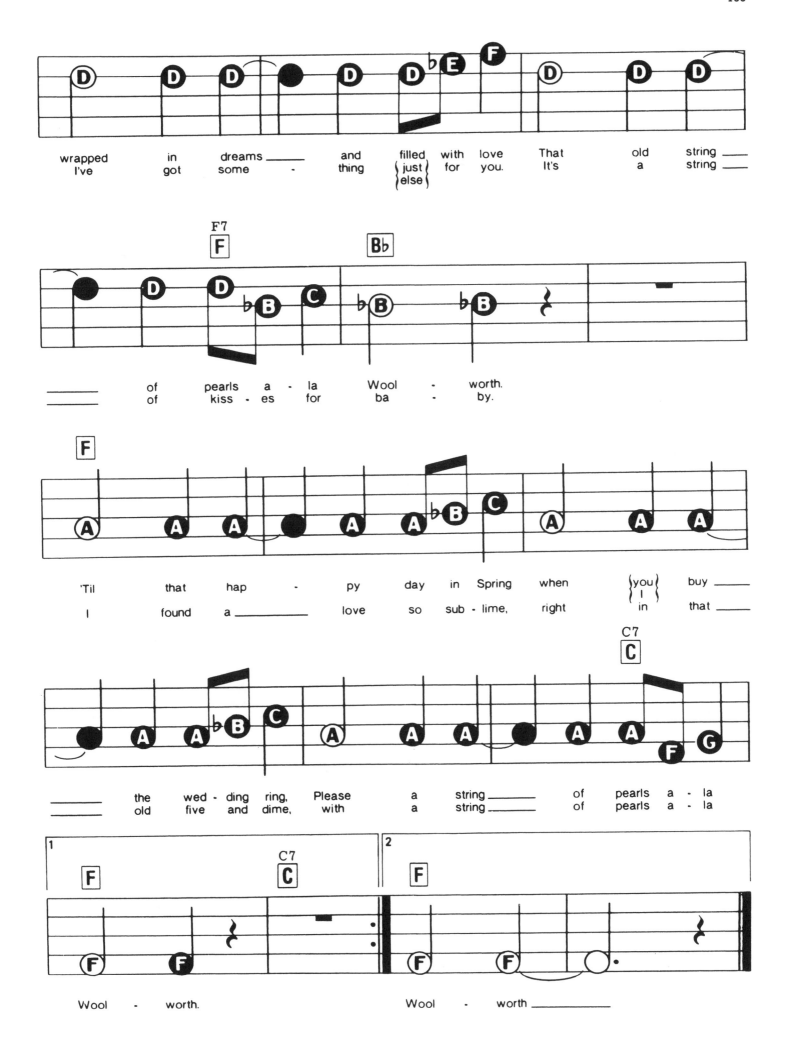

# Tears in Heaven

Registration 8
Rhythm: 8 Beat

Words and Music by Eric Clapton
and Will Jennings

1.,4. Would you know my name _____
2. Would you hold my hand _____
3. *Instrumental*

if I saw you in heav - en?
if I saw you in heav - en?

Would { it / you } be the same _____
Would you help me stand _____

if I saw you in heav - en?
if I saw you in heav - en?

*End instrumental*

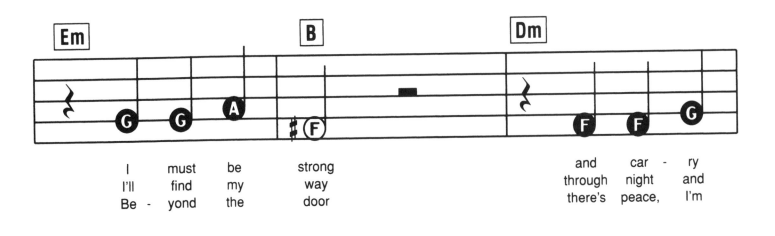

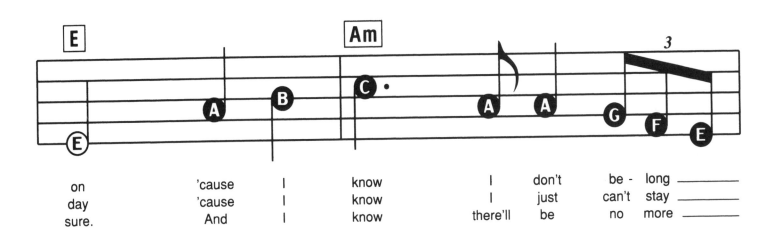

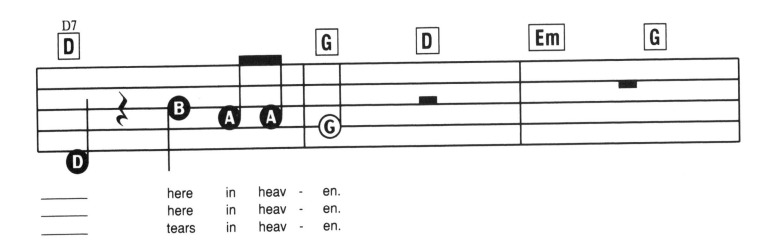

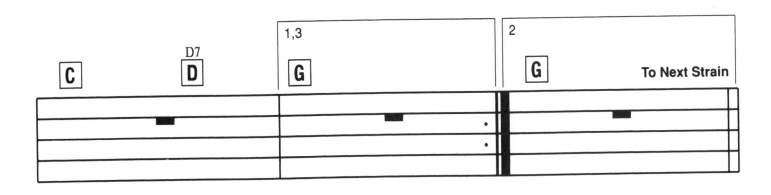

136

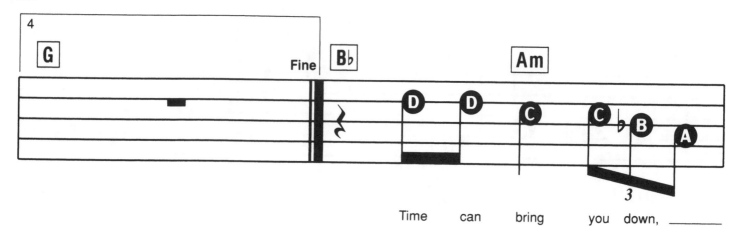

Time can bring you down, _____

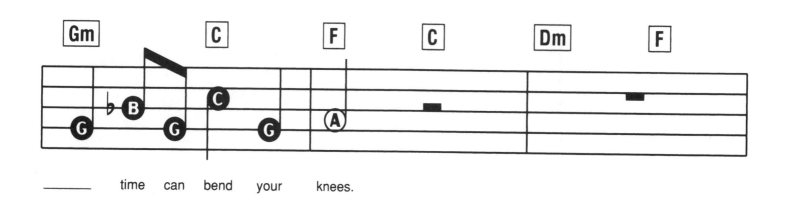

_____ time can bend your knees.

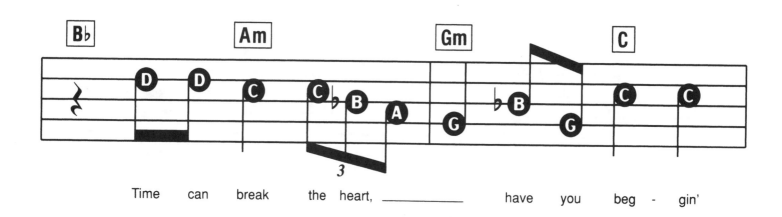

Time can break the heart, _____ have you beg - gin'

**D.C. and Fade**
(Return to beginning
and Fade)

D7

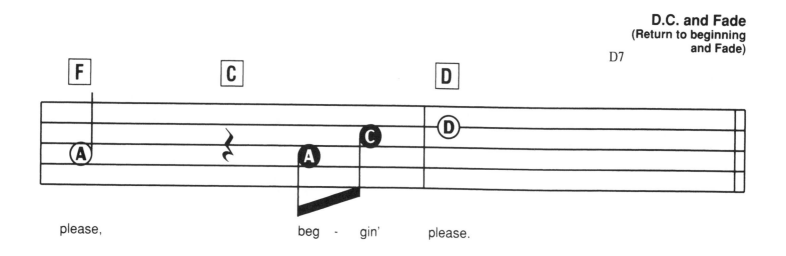

please, beg - gin' please.

# Where Do I Begin
## (Love Theme)
### from the Paramount Picture LOVE STORY

Registration 8
Rhythm: Ballad or Slow Rock

Words by Carl Sigman
Music by Francis Lai

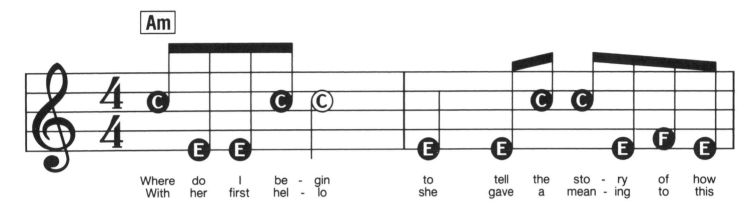

Where do I be-gin to tell the sto-ry of how
With her first hel-lo she gave a mean-ing to this

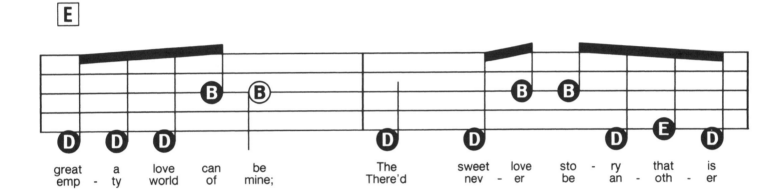

great a love can be The sweet love sto-ry that is
emp-ty world of mine; There'd nev-er be an-oth-er

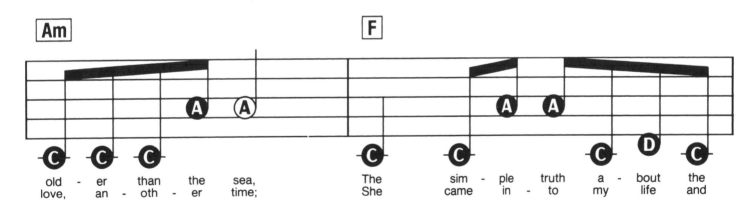

old - er than the sea, The sim-ple truth a-bout the
love, an-oth-er time; She came in-to my life and

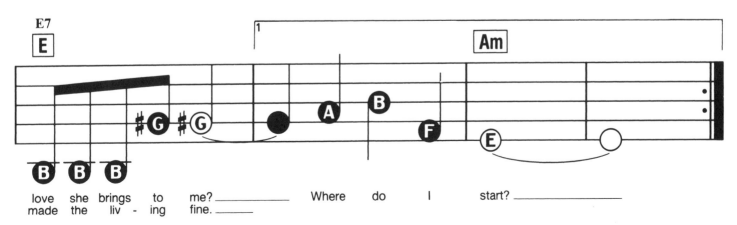

love she brings to me? _____ Where do I start? _____
made the liv-ing fine. _____

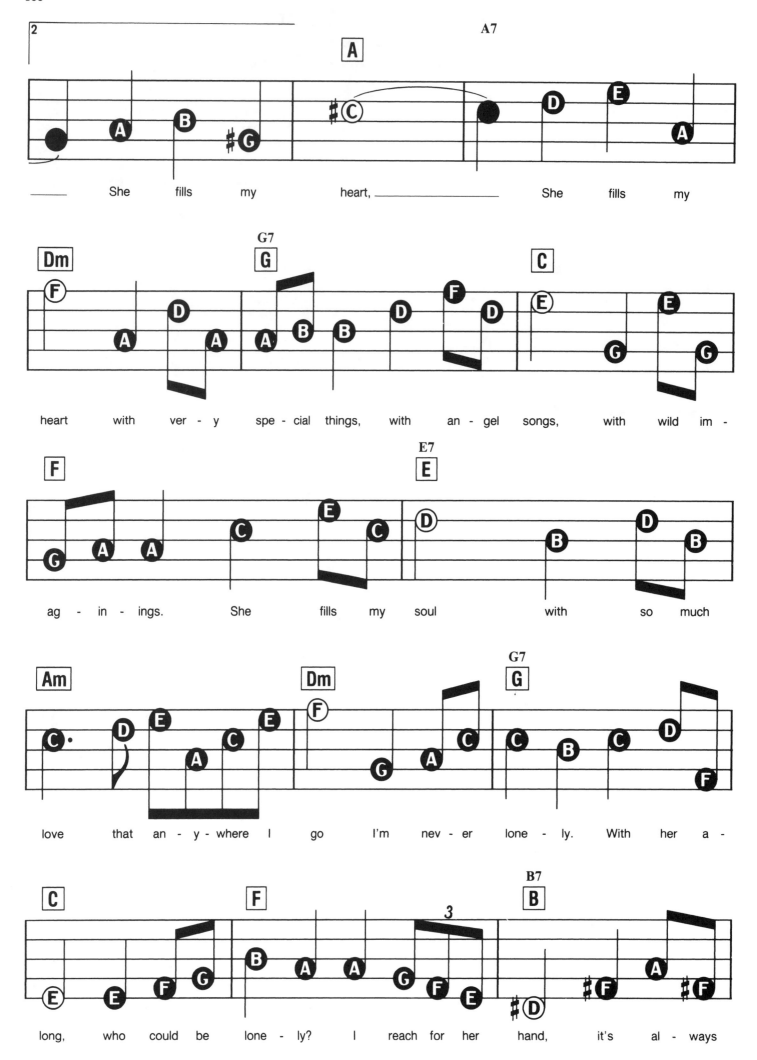

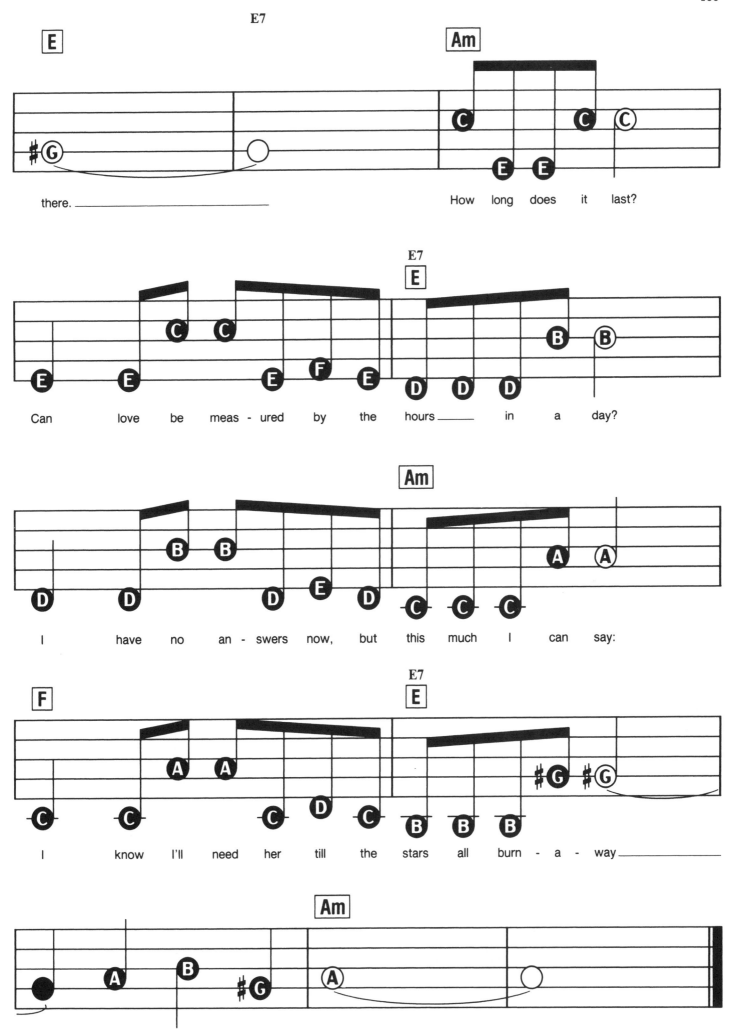

# A Time for Us
## (Love Theme)
### from the Paramount Picture ROMEO AND JULIET

Registration 1
Rhythm: Waltz

Words by Larry Kusik and Eddie Snyder
Music by Nino Rota

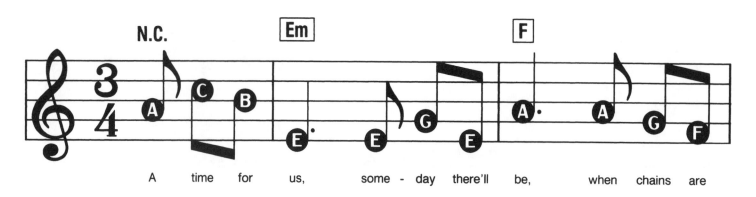

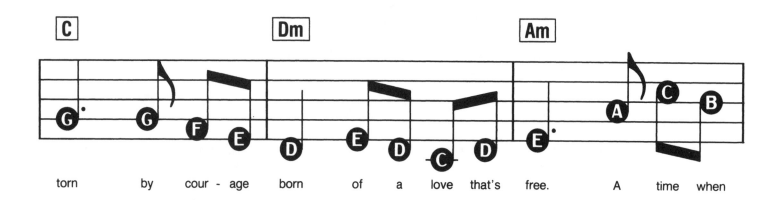

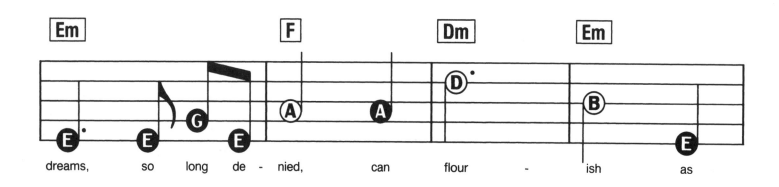

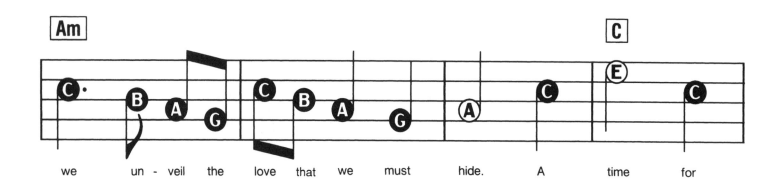

# Time in a Bottle

Registration 8
Rhythm: Waltz

Words and Music by
Jim Croce

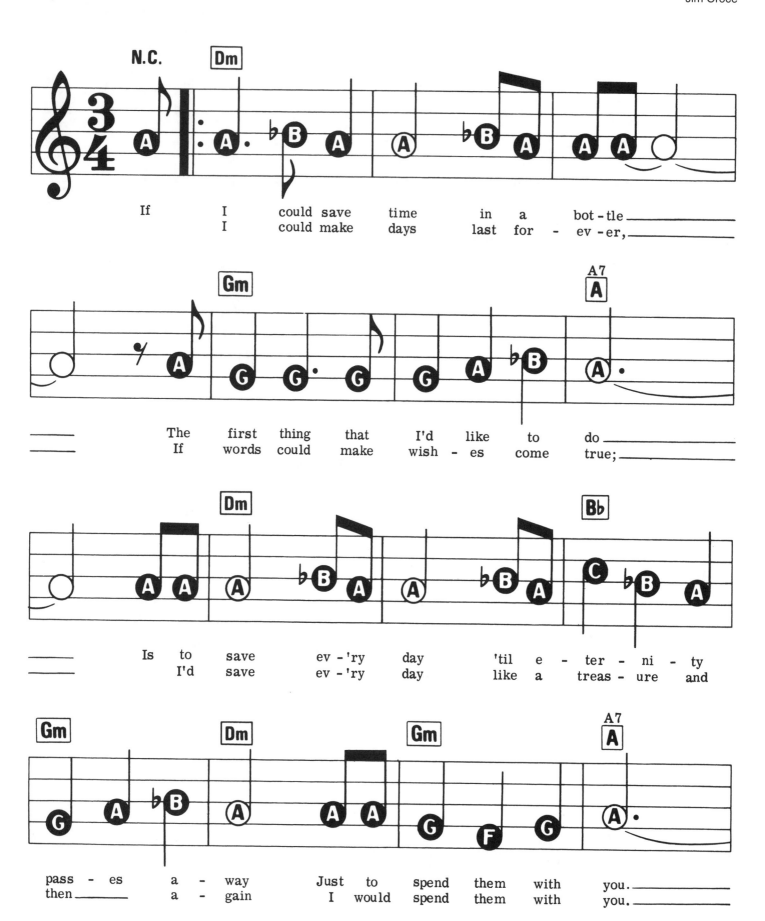

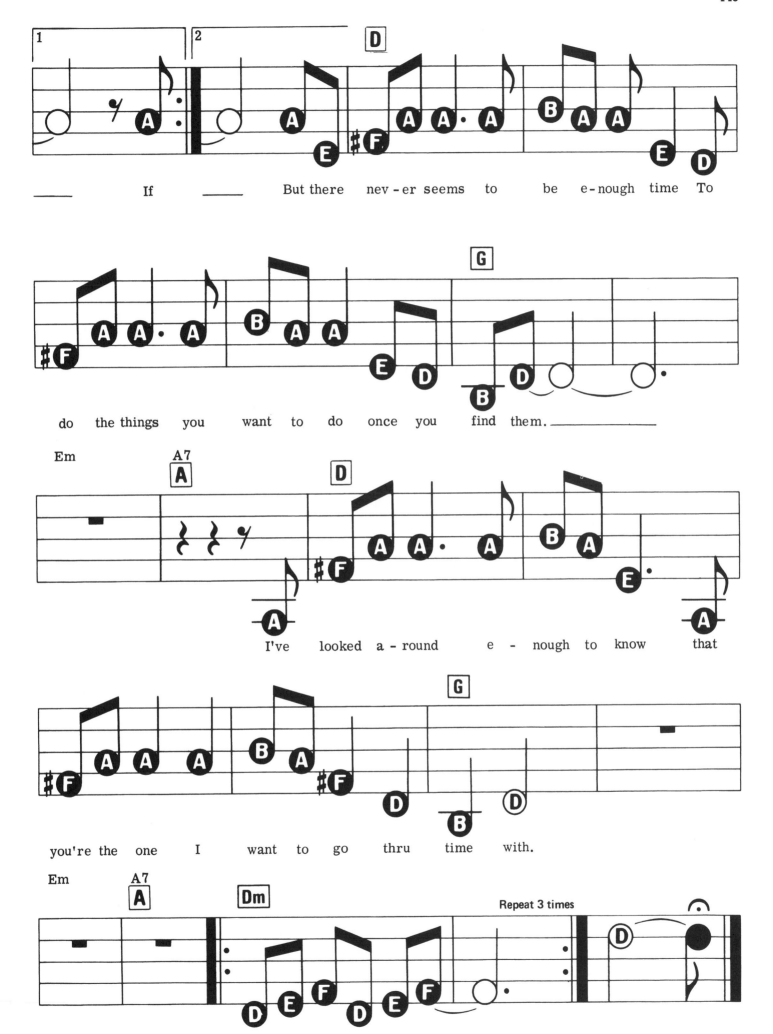

# Top of the World

Registration 2
Rhythm: Fox Trot

Words and Music by John Bettis
and Richard Carpenter

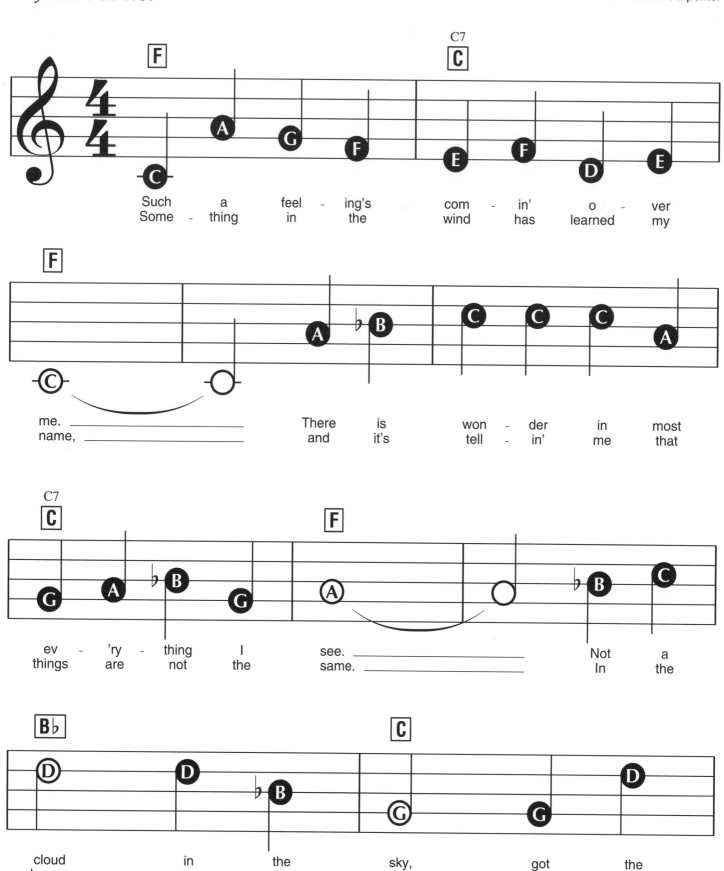

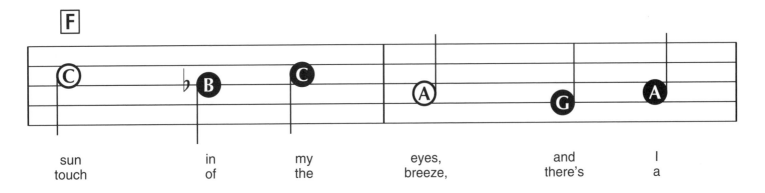

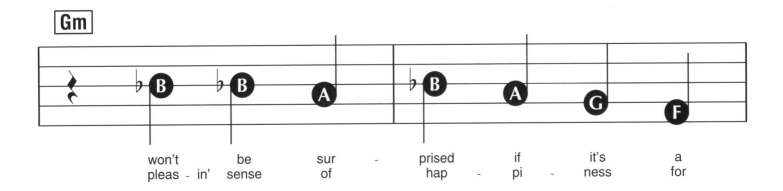

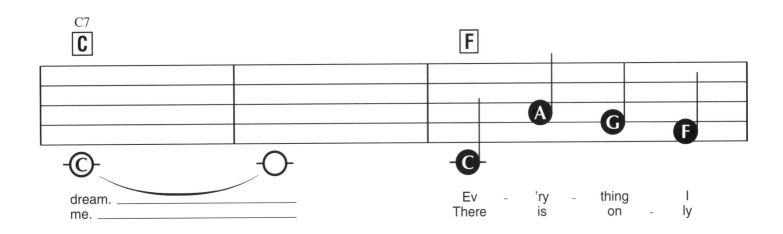

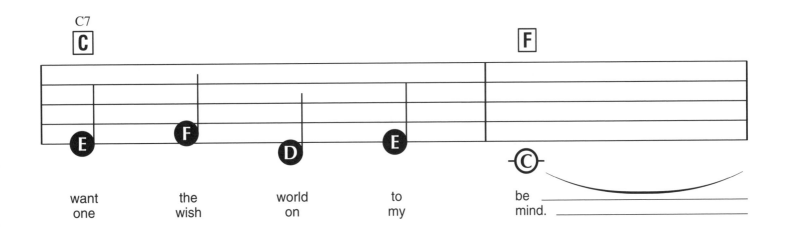

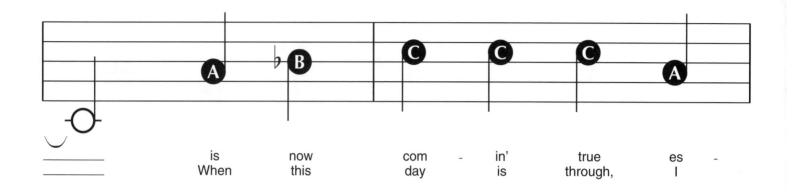

is    now    com - in'    true    es -
When    this    day    is    through,    I

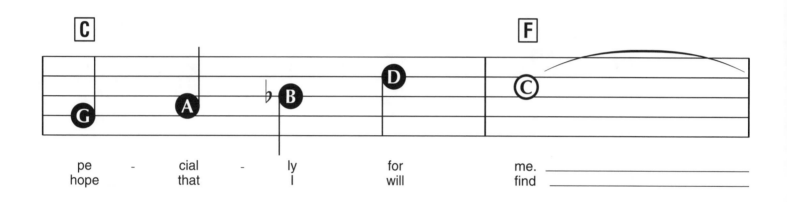

pe - cial - ly    for    me. _____
hope    that    I    will    find _____

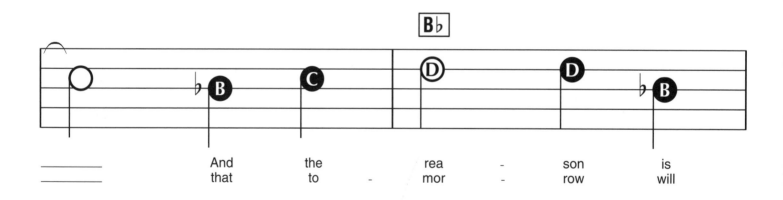

And    the    rea - son    is
that    to - mor - row    will

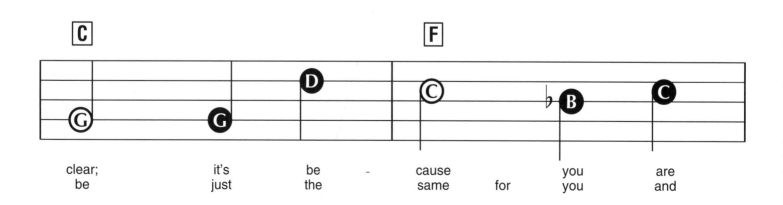

clear;    it's    be - cause    you    are
be    just    be    the    same    for    you    and

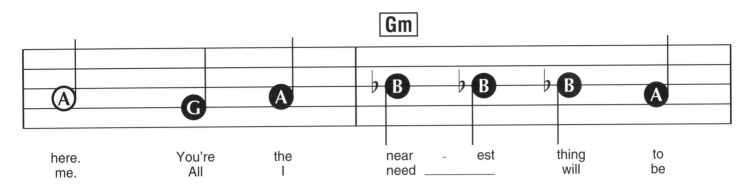

here.
me.
You're
All
the
I
near - est
need _____
thing
will
to
be

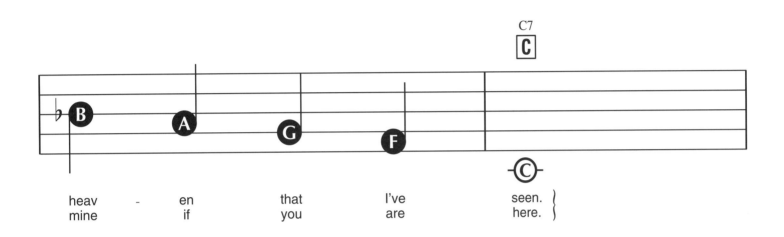

heav - en
mine
that
if
I've
you
seen.
are
here.

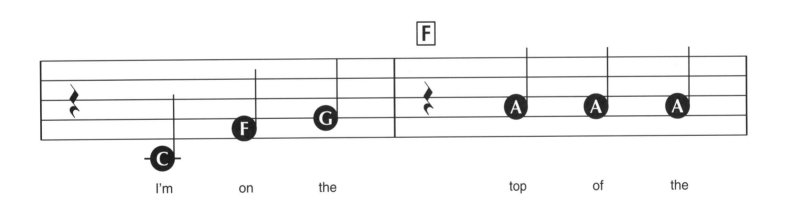

I'm
on
the
top
of
the

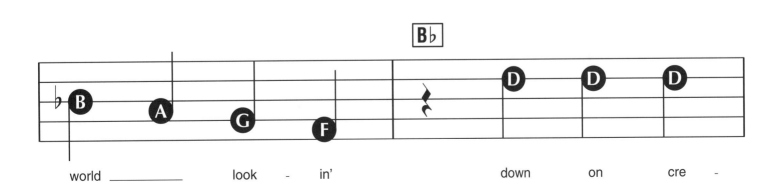

world _____
look - in'
down
on
cre -

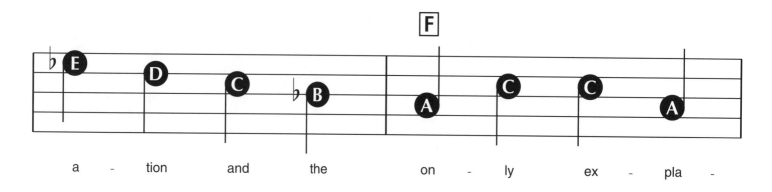

a - tion and the on - ly ex - pla -

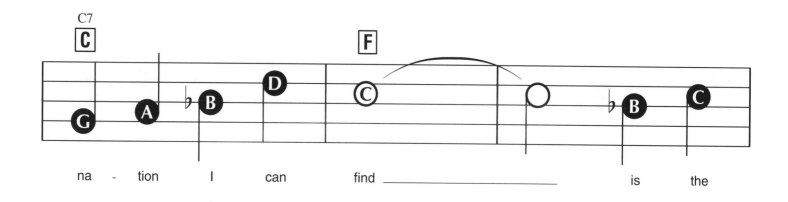

na - tion I can find _____ is the

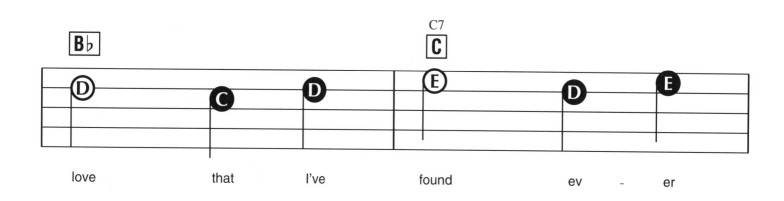

love that I've found ev - er

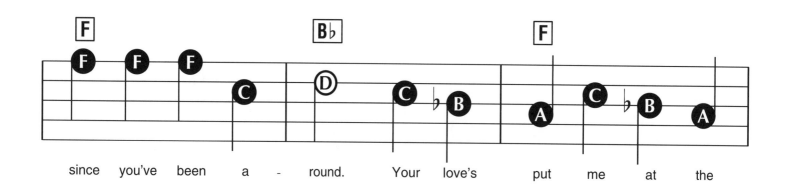

since you've been a - round. Your love's put me at the

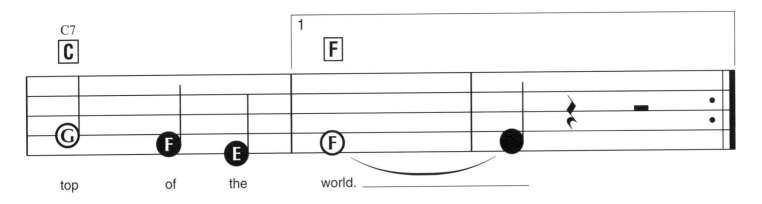

top        of        the        world.

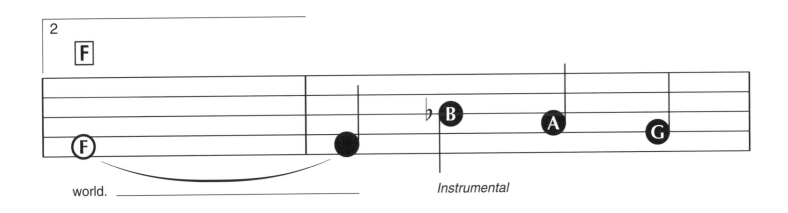

world.        Instrumental

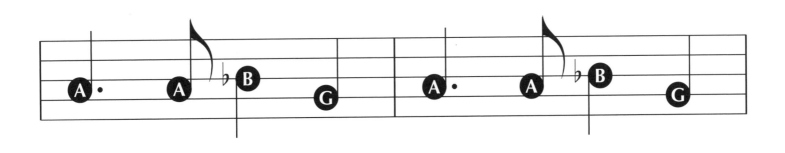

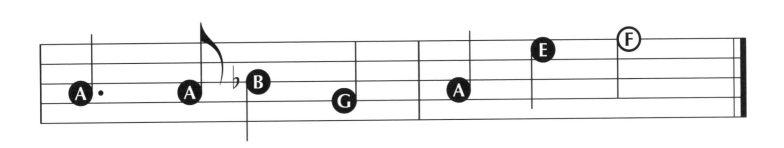

# Unchained Melody
### from the Motion Picture UNCHAINED

Registration 4
Rhythm: Ballad

Lyric by Hy Zaret
Music by Alex North

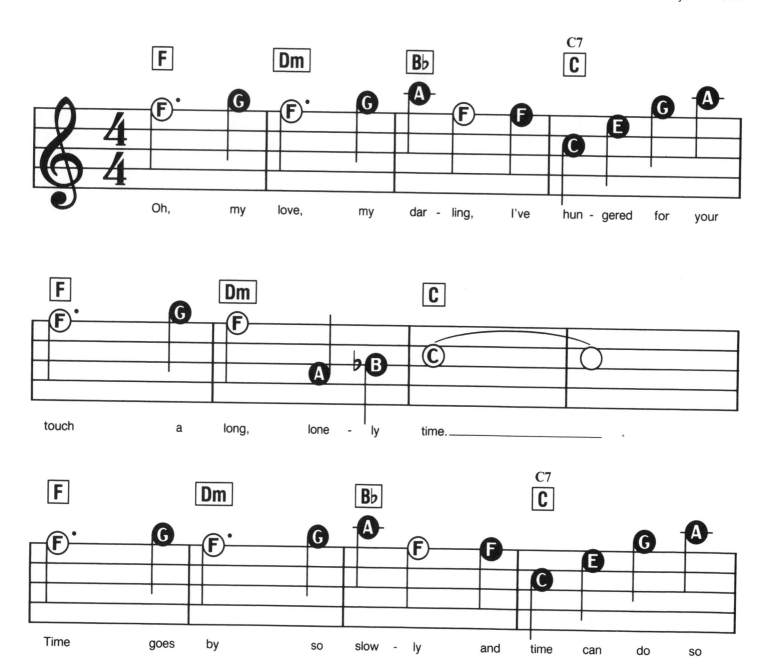

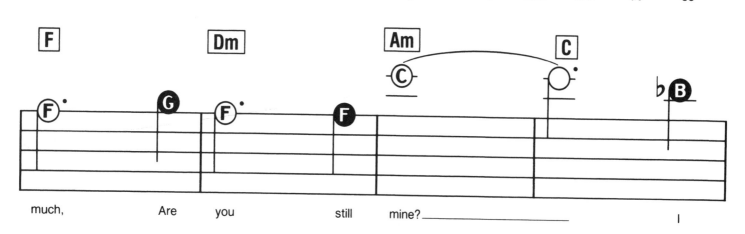

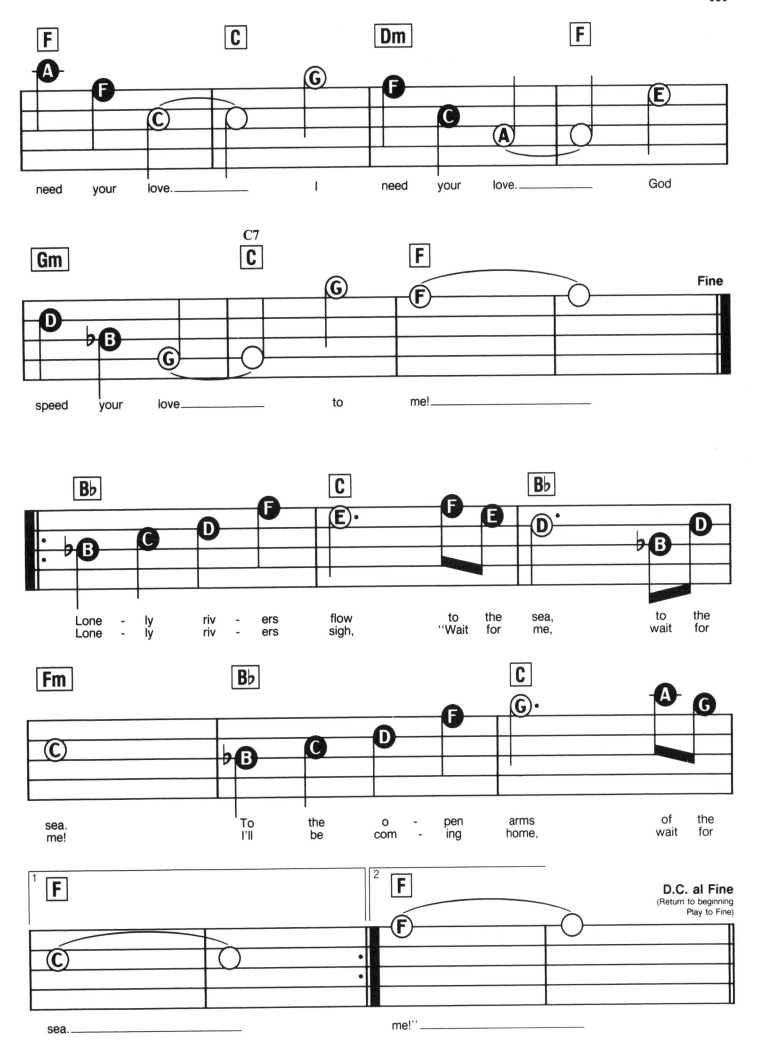

# Unforgettable

Registration 3
Rhythm: Fox Trot or Swing

Words and Music by
Irving Gordon

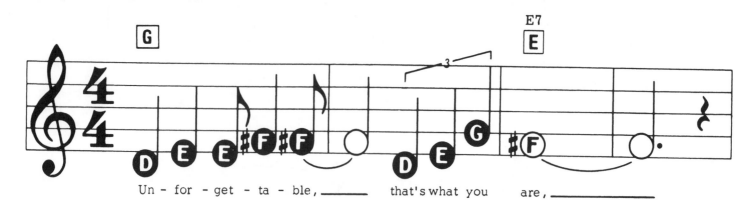

Un - for - get - ta - ble, _____ that's what you are, _____

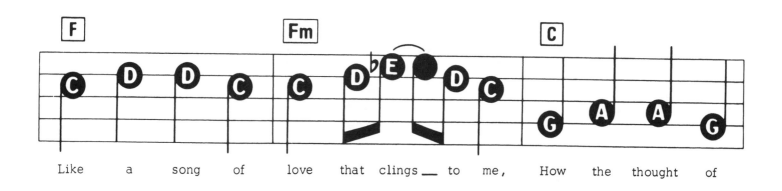

Un - for - get - ta - ble, _____ though near or far, _____

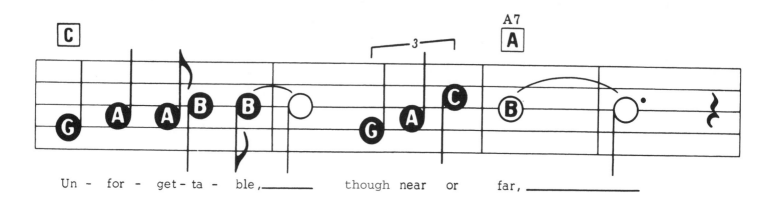

Like a song of love that clings __ to me, How the thought of

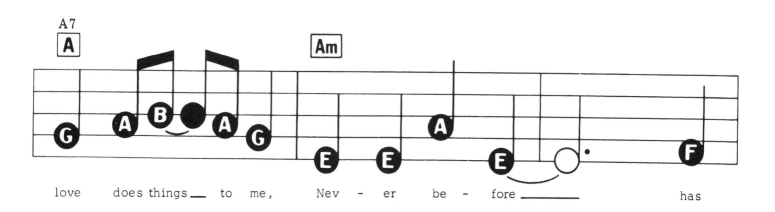

love does things __ to me, Nev - er be - fore _____ has

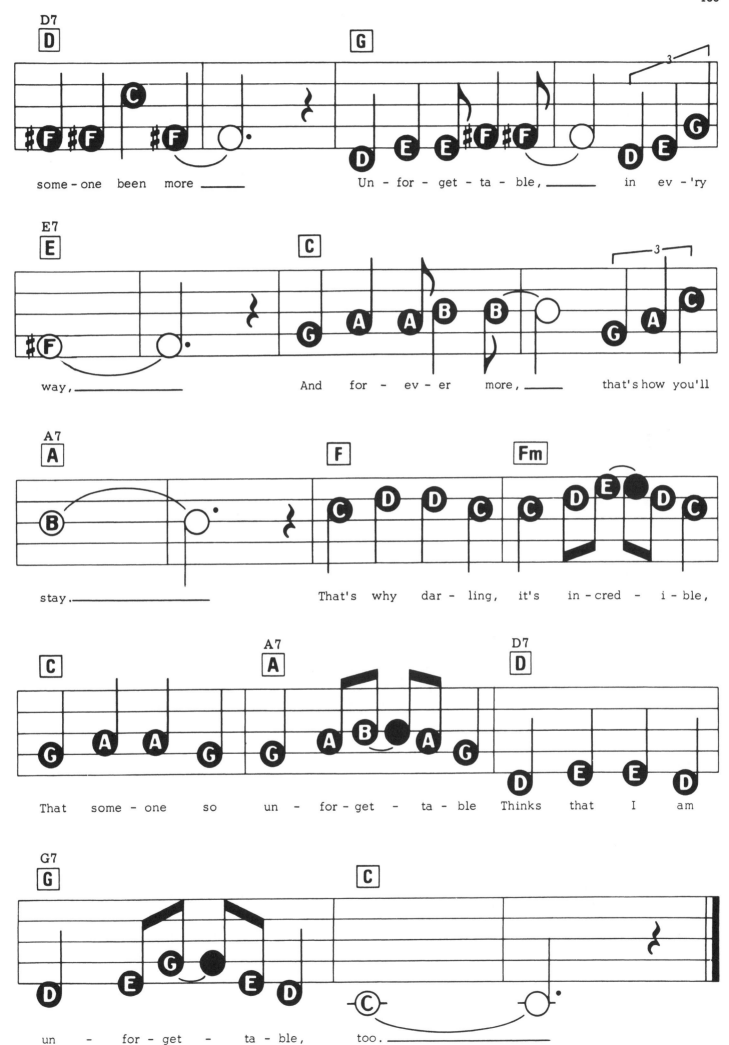

# The Way We Were
### from the Motion Picture THE WAY WE WERE

Registration 8
Rhythm: Slow Rock or Ballad

Words by Alan and Marilyn Bergman
Music by Marvin Hamlisch

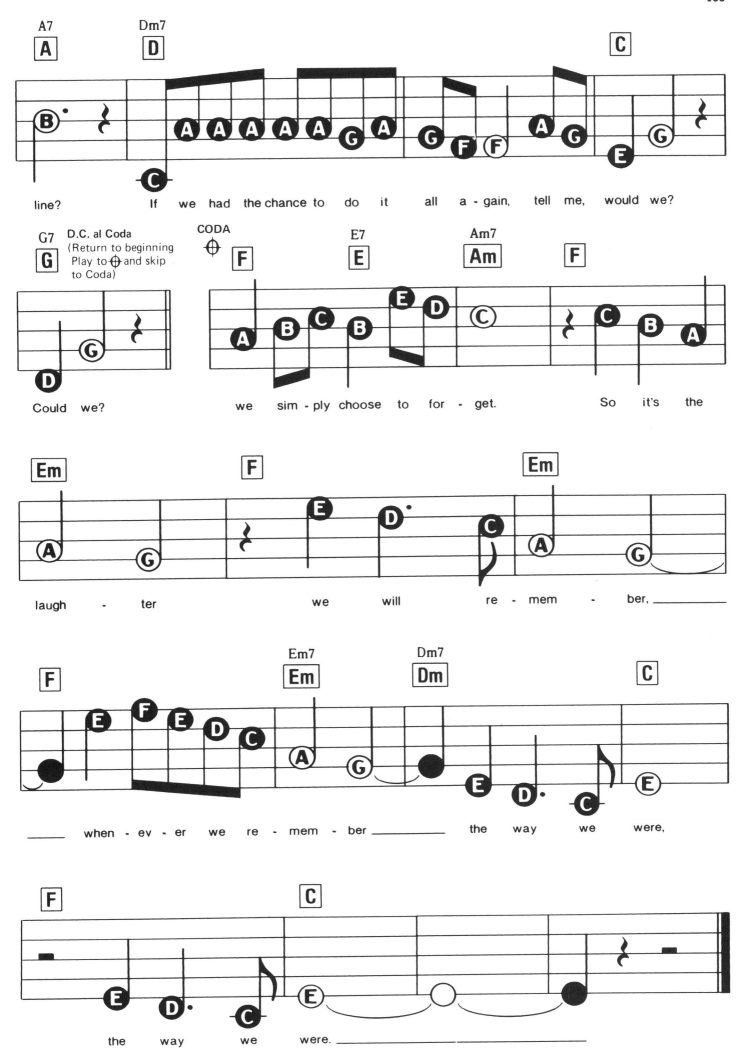

# We've Only Just Begun

Registration 1
Rhythm: 8 Beat or Pops

Words and Music by Roger Nichols
and Paul Williams

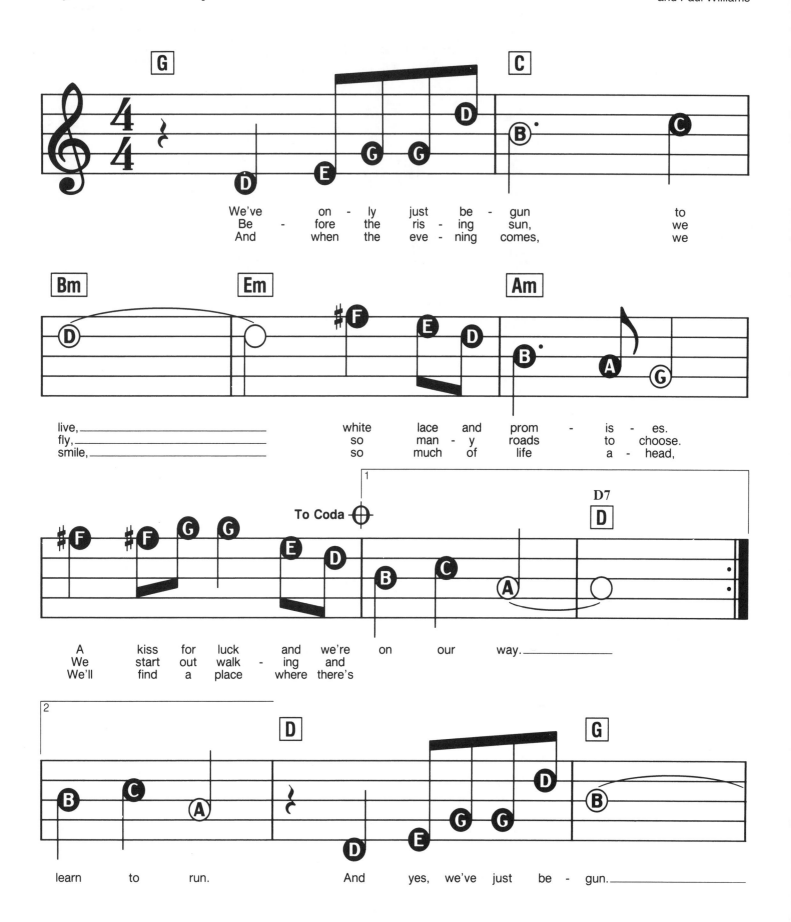

157

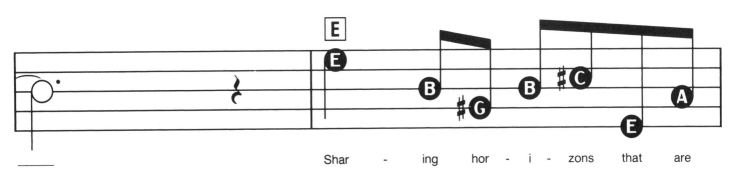

Shar - ing hor - i - zons that are

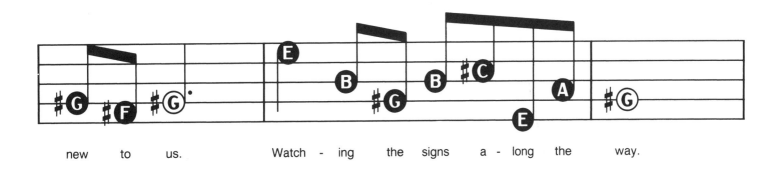

new to us. Watch - ing the signs a - long the way.

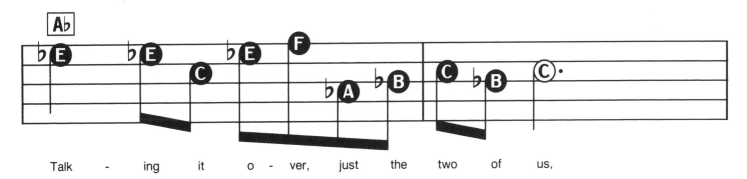

Talk - ing it o - ver, just the two of us,

**D.C. al Coda**
(Return to beginning
Play to ⊕ and
skip to Coda)

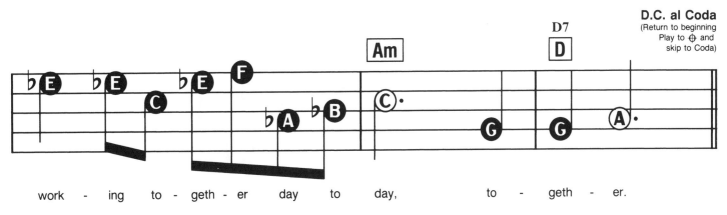

work - ing to - geth - er day to day, to - geth - er.

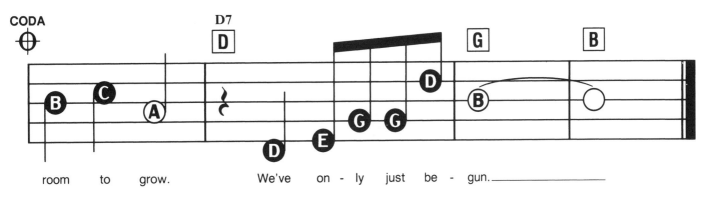

room to grow. We've on - ly just be - gun.

# What a Wonderful World

Registration 2
Rhythm: Ballad

Words and Music by George David Weiss
and Bob Thiele

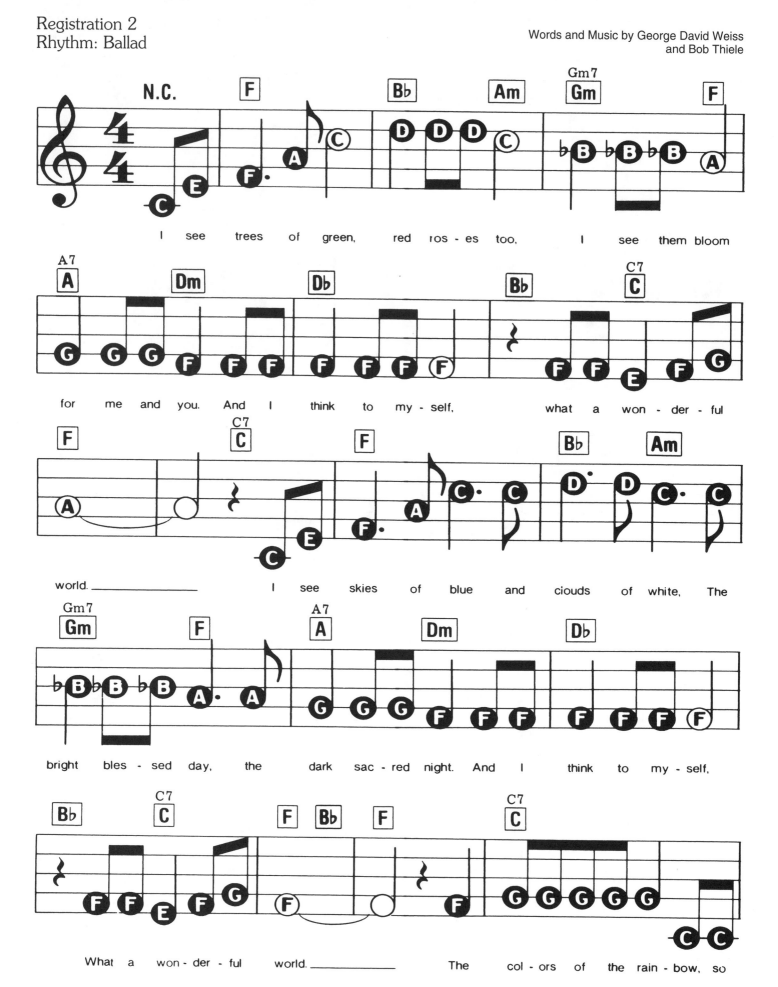

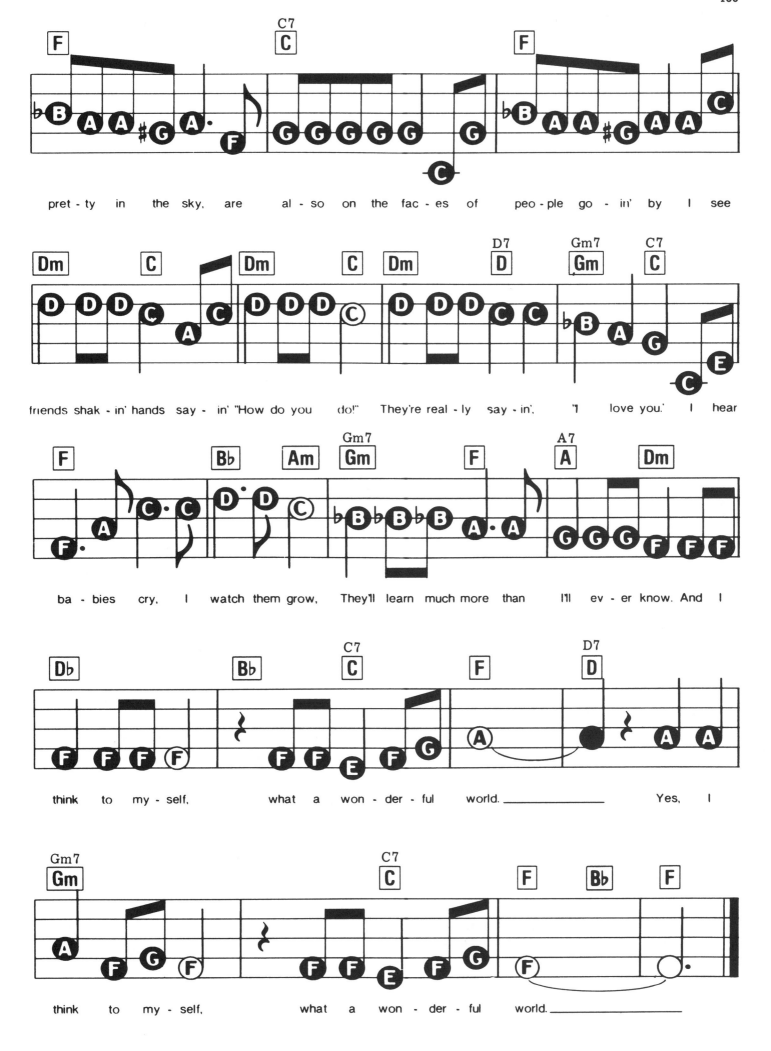

# What Kind of Fool Am I?

## from the Musical Production STOP THE WORLD – I WANT TO GET OFF

Registration 2
Rhythm: Fox Trot

Words and Music by Leslie Bricusse
and Anthony Newley

What kind of fool am I, _____ who nev - er
lips are these, _____ that lied with

fell in love _____ It seems that I'm the on - ly
ev - 'ry kiss? _____ That whis - pered

one that I have been think - ing of. _____ What kind of {man}{life} is this? _____

An em - pty shell, _____ A lone - ly

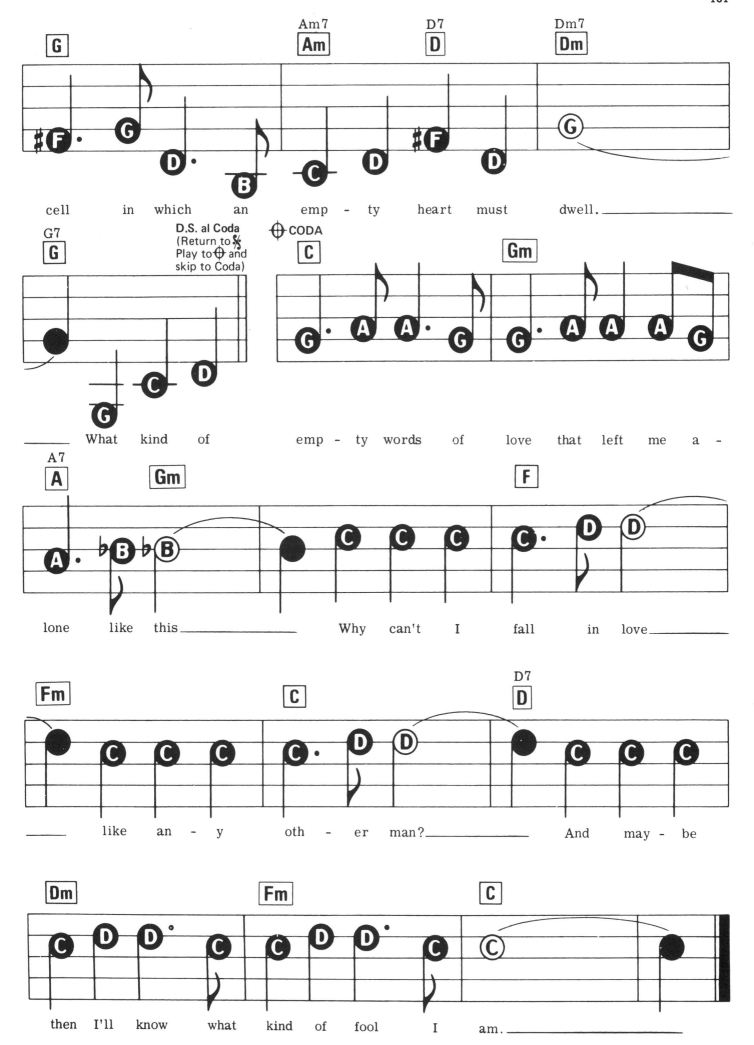

# When I Fall in Love
## from ONE MINUTE TO ZERO

Registration 10
Rhythm: Fox Trot or Swing

Words by Edward Heyman
Music by Victor Young

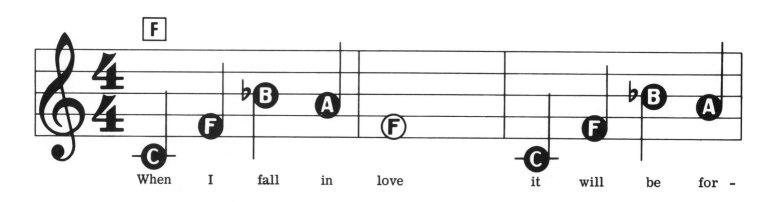

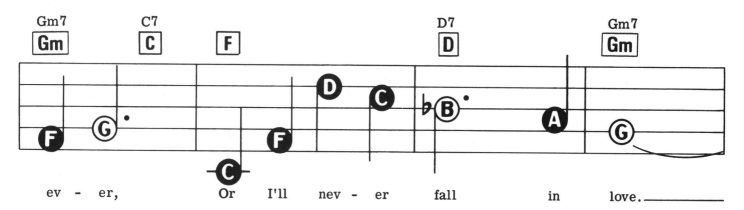

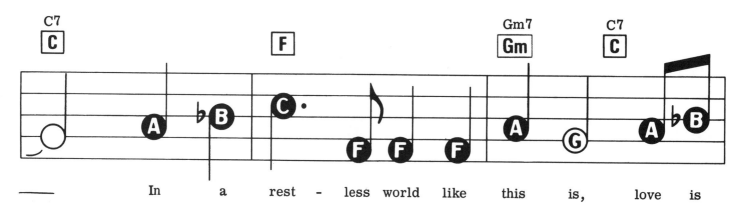

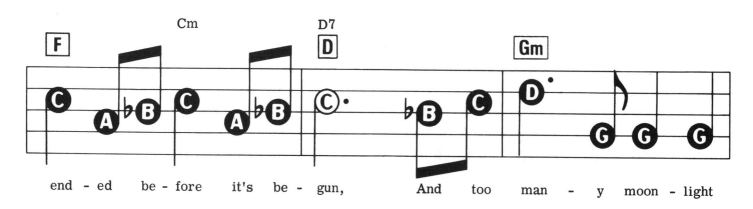

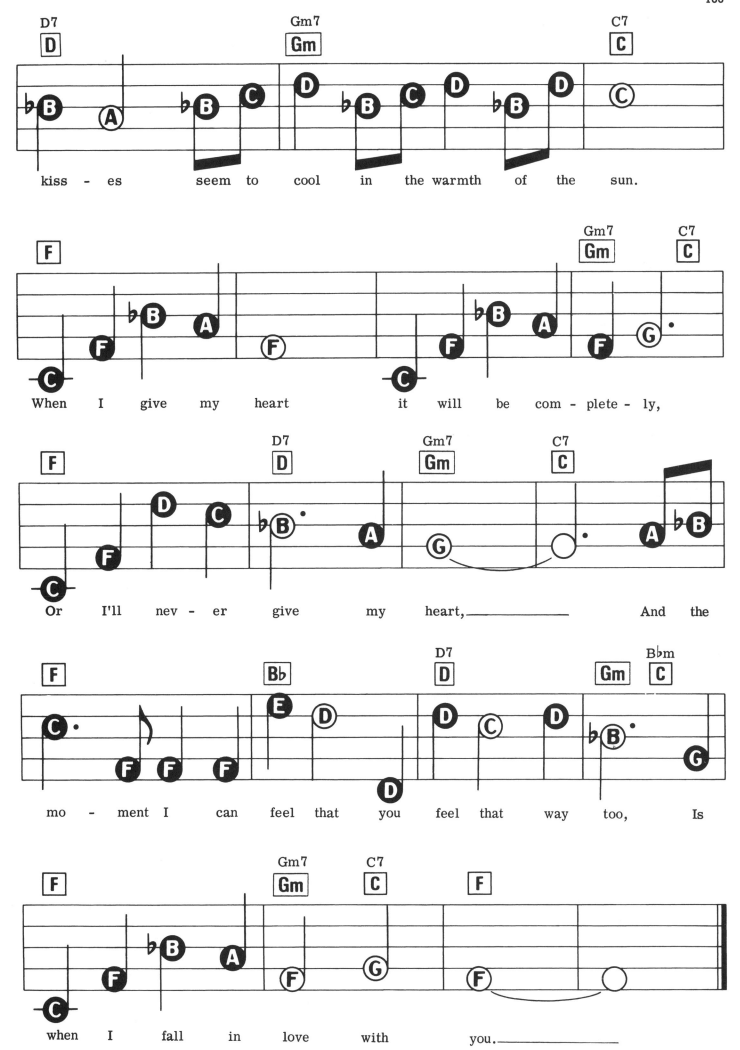

# When You Wish Upon a Star

**Registration 1**
**Rhythm: Ballad**

Words by Ned Washington
Music by Leigh Harline

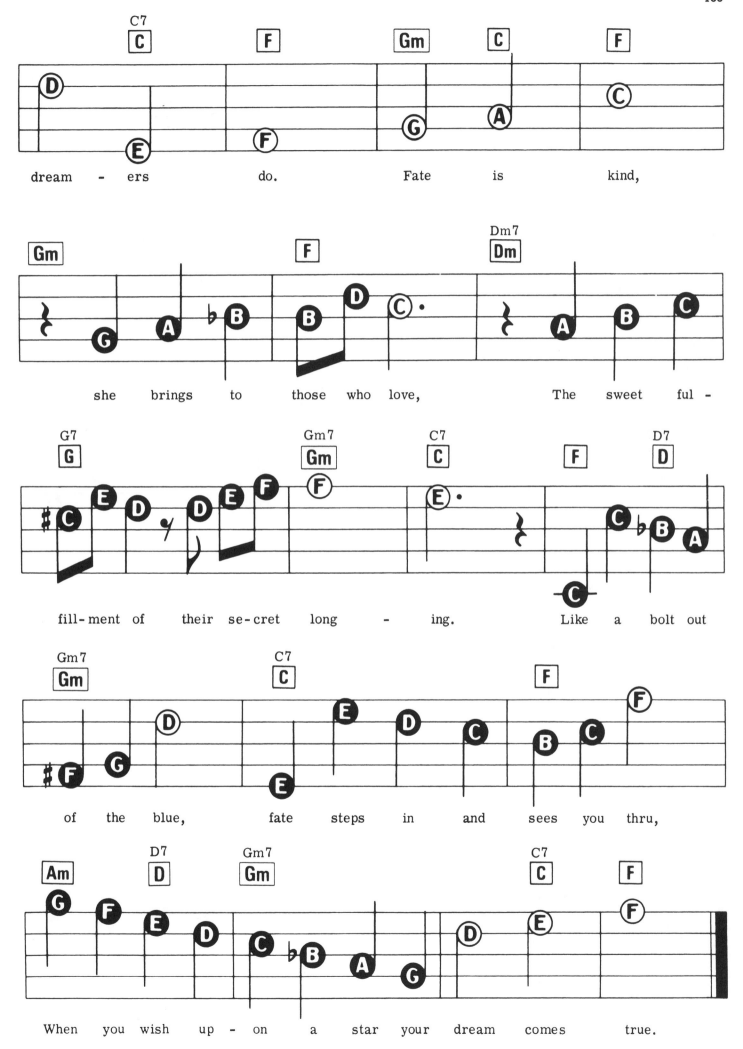

# Yesterday

Registration 2
Rhythm: Rock or Ballad

Words and Music by John Lennon
and Paul McCartney

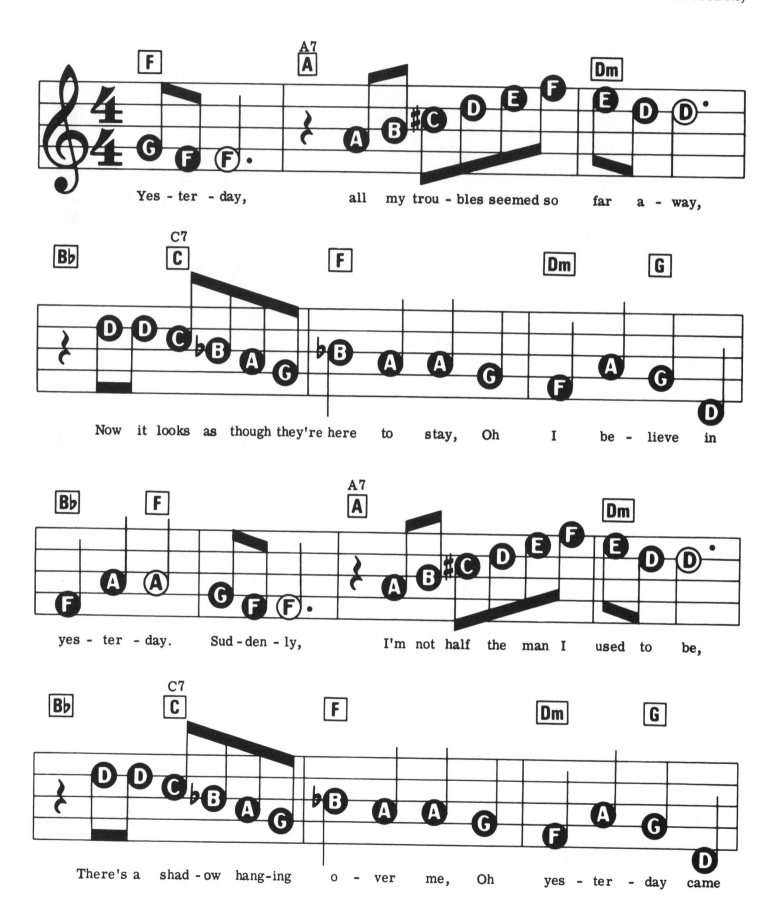

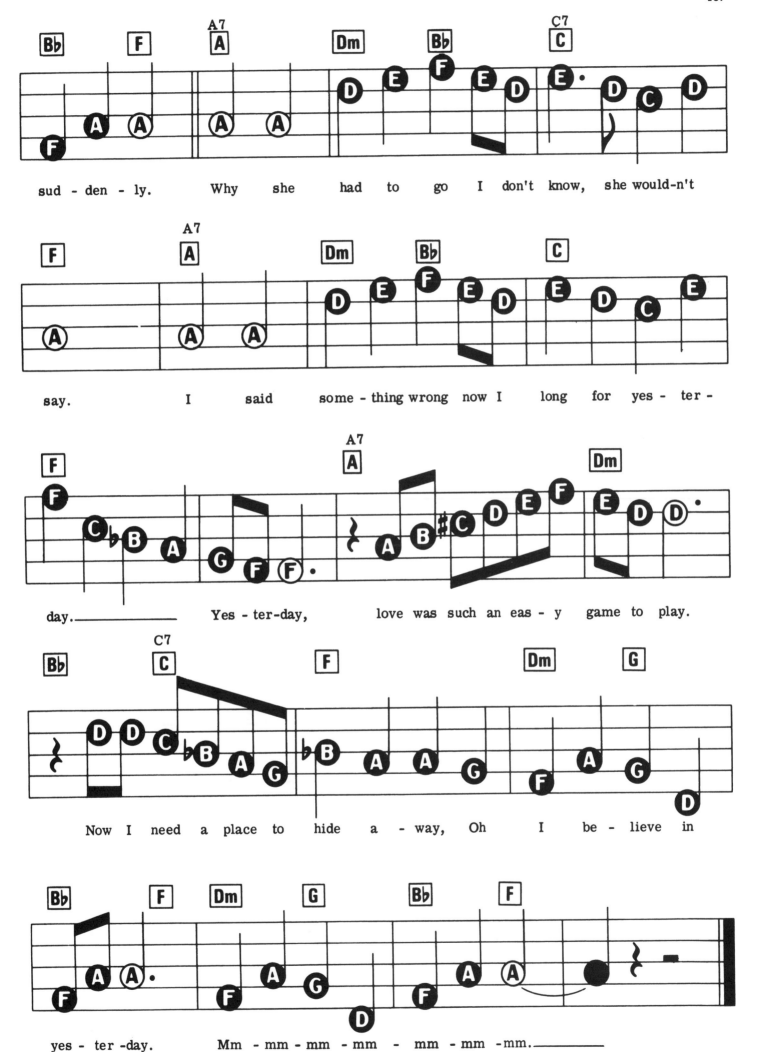

# You Are So Beautiful

Registration 1
Rhythm: Pops or 8 Beat

Words and Music by Billy Preston
and Bruce Fisher

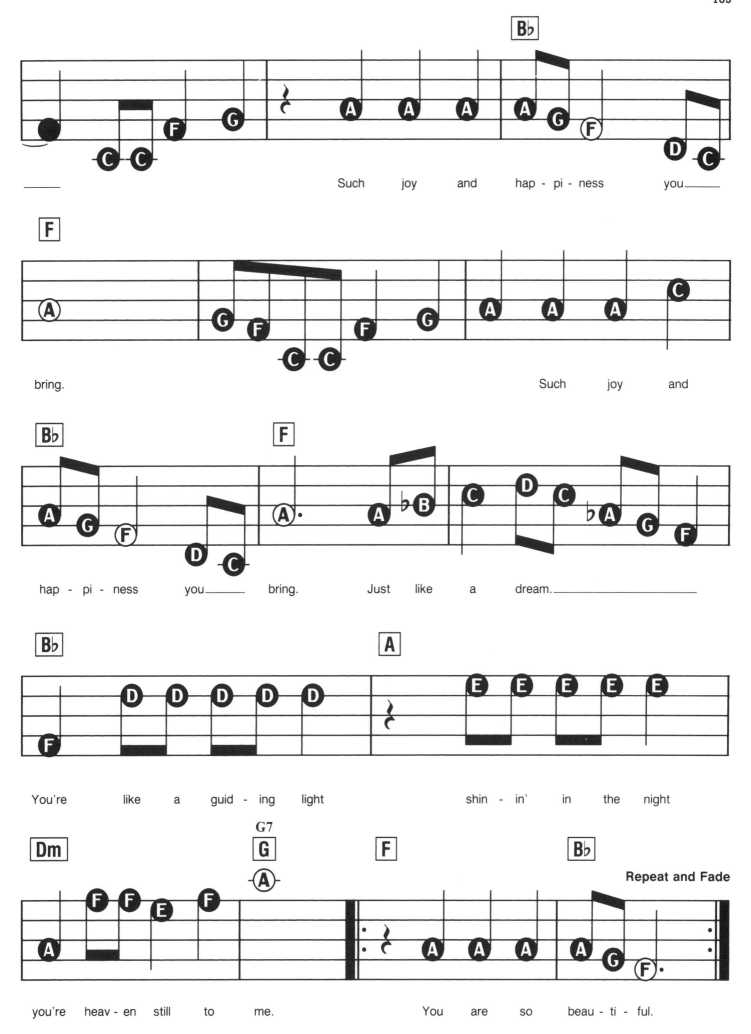

# You Are the Sunshine of My Life

Registration 7
Rhythm: 8 Beat or Bossa Nova

Words and Music by
Stevie Wonder

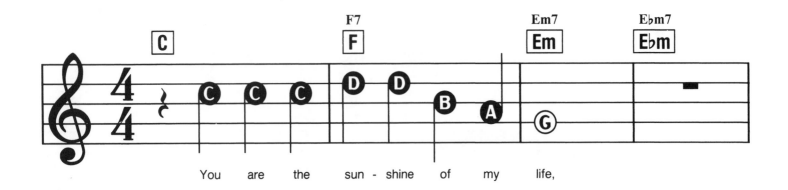

You are the sun - shine of my life,

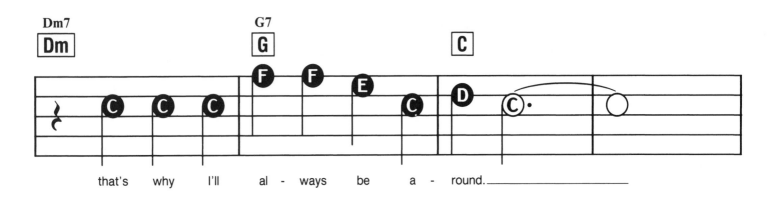

that's why I'll al - ways be a - round._____

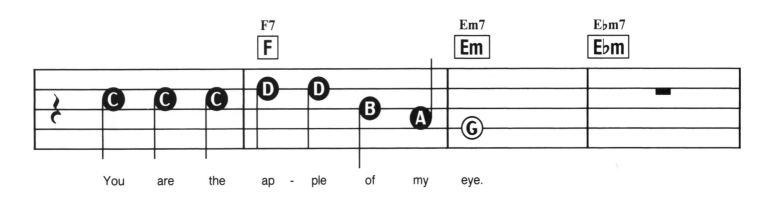

You are the ap - ple of my eye.

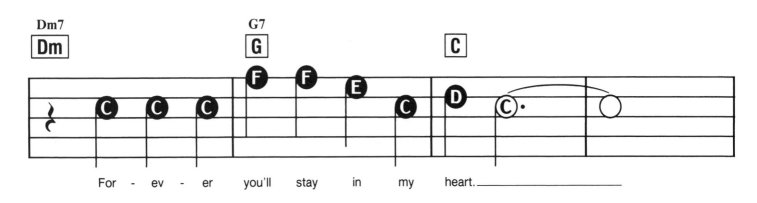

For - ev - er you'll stay in my heart._____

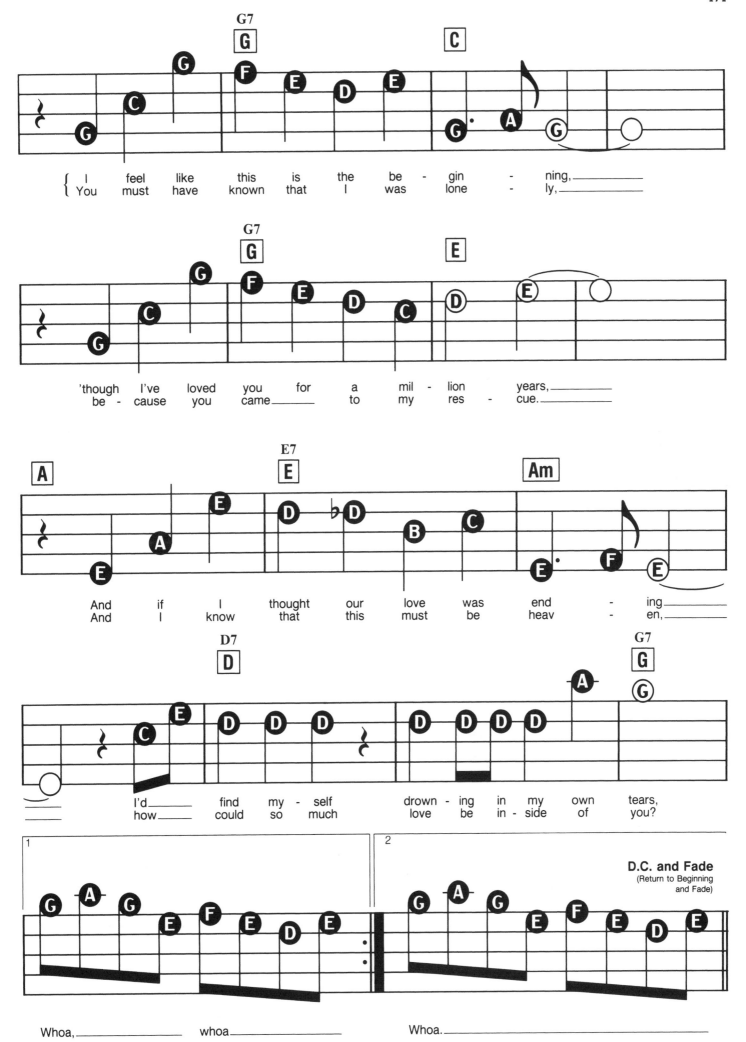

# A Whole New World
## (Aladdin's Theme)
### from Walt Disney's ALADDIN

Registration 1
Rhythm: 8 Beat or Pops

Music by Alan Menken
Lyrics by Tim Rice

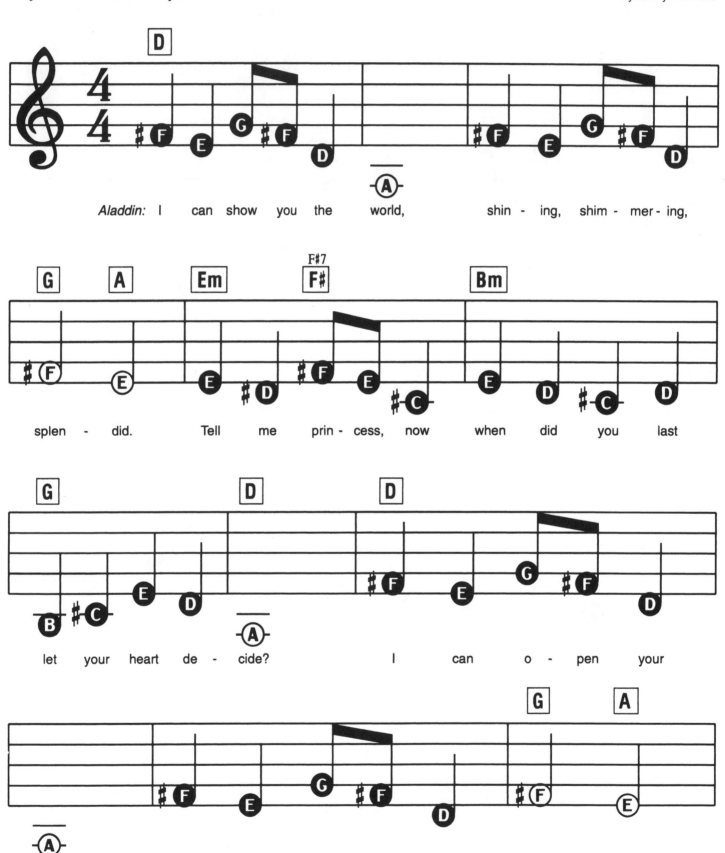

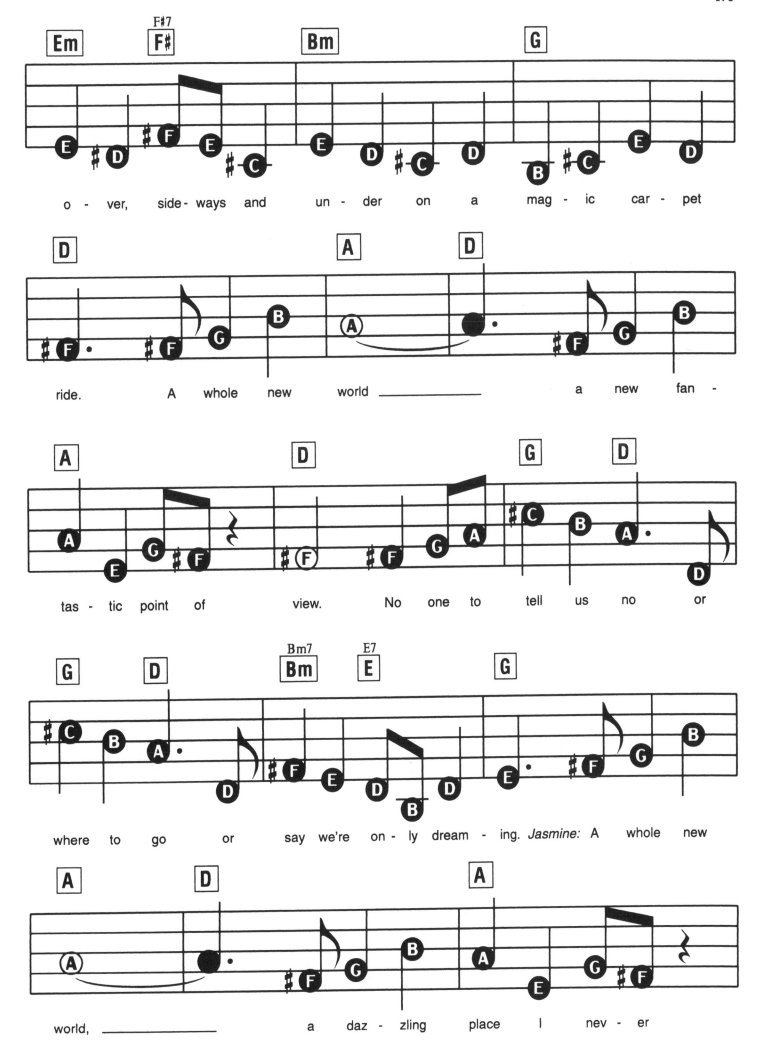

174

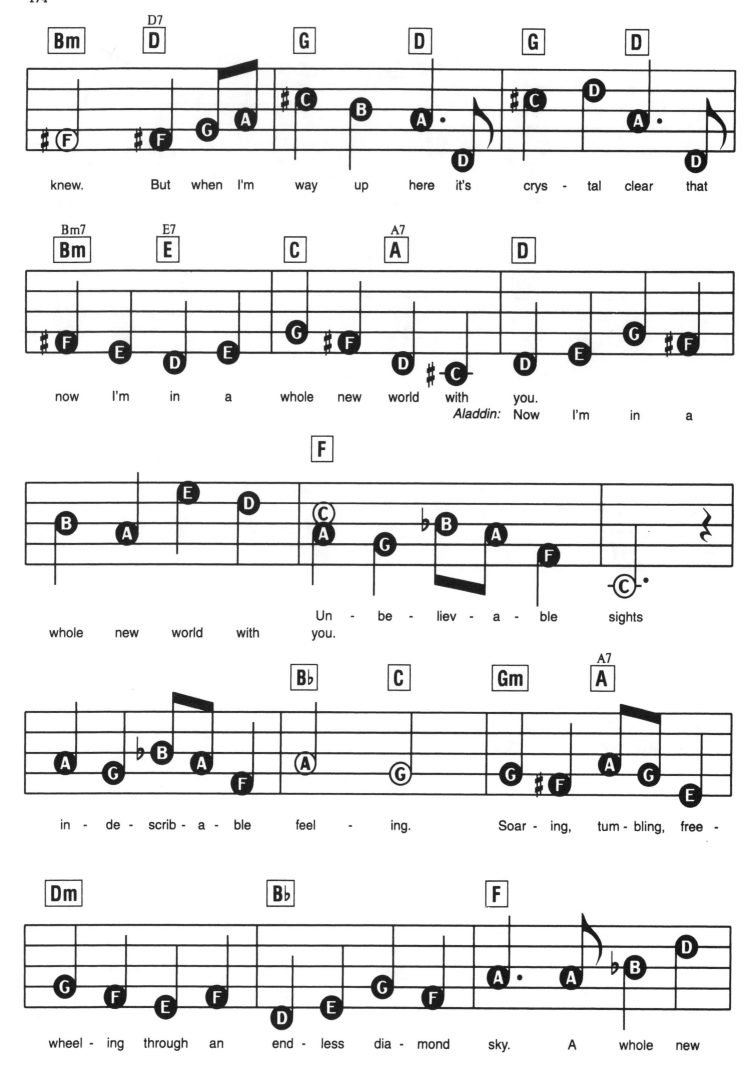

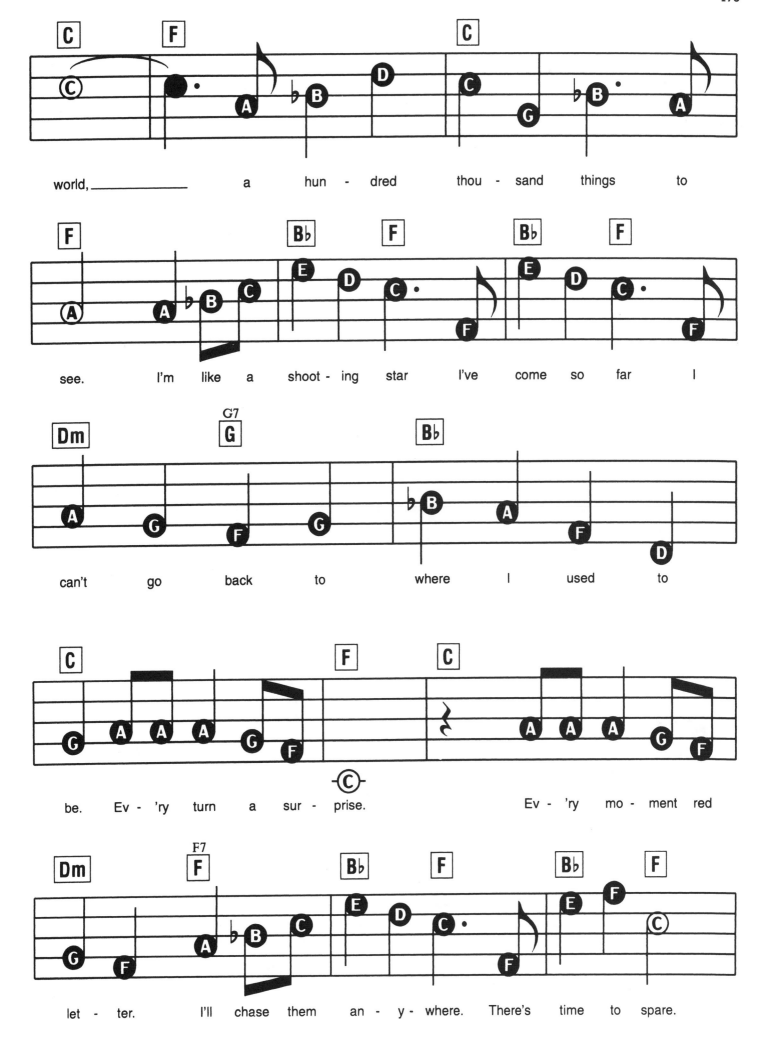

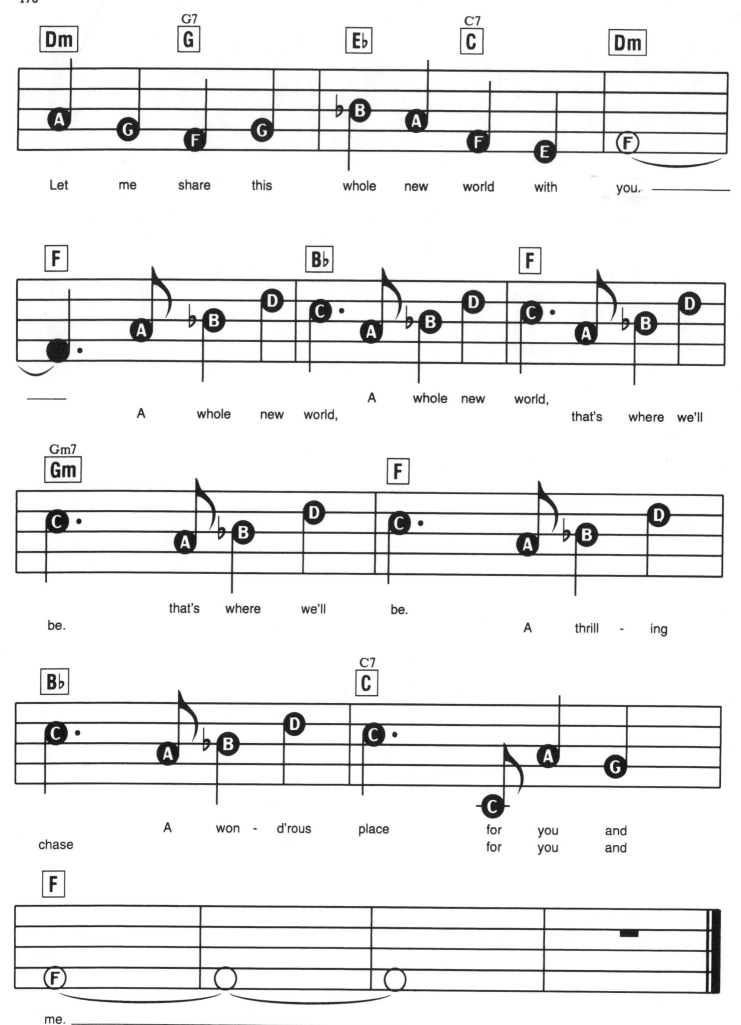